THE SQUARE WHEEL

Do you believe in square wheels?

Colin Campbell-Barker

Contents

✦═══✦

Chapter 1

Do you believe in Square wheels?

It is said that the wheel is perhaps the greatest invention of all time. This simple invention took **common sense** to be designed, used and developed! This simplistic idea is almost the definition of sound thought. So just like the invention of the wheel it is also vitally important to use common sense and sound thought when evaluating the greater questions about this life. But when doing so, many people take this great, simple, effective and logical idea of a round wheel and turn it into a square one.

Say if someone approached you along the street and said "Look at my new bike! It's great. Check out the square wheels; they work much better than my old bikes round wheels."

I'm sure you would think this individual was very confused indeed. You would intuitively know that their square wheeled bicycle was utter **mechanical nonsense**, because a round wheeled bike makes total sense.....which is the truth full stop. Maybe some of us would ask them to explain why they would want to use a bike with square wheels instead of round ones. If you saw multitudes of people trying to ride such bikes I'm sure you would want to help them, and find out why they think this is logical. So it is down to a person's knowledge and understanding through experience in life that would stop someone insanely trying to convince you that square wheels are better than round ones. It is simply a matter of sense Vs nonsense, sanity Vs insanity, and truth Vs lies. So reasoning using common sense clearly shows a square wheel is a ridiculous idea. The sound and logical idea of a round wheel is painfully obvious.

Many people are trying to use square wheels - as far as questions and beliefs in life go. So people have 'square wheels' (beliefs and theories) in their minds that if examined and viewed properly would show they do not work at all. So let's now apply these same principles to bigger questions we face in life.

Sometimes things that don't work may seem as though they do if viewed from a single perspective:

Out of the two wheels which one is round and which one is square? They both look the same from this view-point; no one can know which one is which. From this limited angle it seems as though they are both round and that they might both work equally well.

This way of seeing things can be applied in other issues that can be much more important, where it is vital to examine the whole picture from all angles.

Looking at the wheels in this way shows that lies or misconceptions can appear to be truthful so we can be fooled into seeing an issue from this deceptive angle and think it is right because that's all we were taught.

By now you must be wondering what it is that you think about in daily life that relates to the wheels? With these thoughts in mind let's look at some important issues - issues that affect our whole concept of life.

For starters evolution (which is the **theory** that life evolved, or just happened).Also the 'Big Bang' (which is the **theory** that the universe began by a big explosion). These theories are exactly like the square wheel. They simply do not work at all: here's
how and why:

Chapter 2

Evolution (The evil solution)

We all know about D.N.A, the building code of life. (Just in case you don't, D.N.A is found in you and all life because it is a massive instruction code or 'blue print' that enables life to grow into all it's different and complex designs. So the shape and structure of your whole body and all the workings of it are coded in your D.N.A!)

So D.N.A holds an incredible amount of very complex data or information that all fits together to enable the construction and growth of a human being, and all life. The main building blocks, as it were, that D.N.A uses to build life are called cells. Cells are tiny complex structures that 'house' D.N.A. (D.N.A stands for: Deoxyribonucleic acid.)

D.N.A is a giant biological 'factory' that is fully automated. It can work or run on its own like a enormous computer program, which makes it even more complicated and amazing. This giant biological 'factory' produces all kinds of building blocks (cells) and instructs and uses it's massive 'information bank' to make all life. D.N.A is a fully automated biological 'factory' that works unaided because it has been **designed** to work that way.

Keep in mind this next piece about a wheel not being able to make another wheel (obviously) as it relates to cells without the use of D.N.A.

If you wanted two new wheels for your bike, would you buy only one wheel then wait for it to make a copy of itself? Of course not! That is utter nonsense. Instead you would go and buy two wheels that were both crafted and made in a factory by skilled, knowledgeable designers and craftsmen. But unfortunately people accept and believe that the ridiculous concept of one wheel making another is possible! Because like the bike wheels one cell cannot produce another cell without D.N.A. Only the 'factory' (D.N.A) has the information and instruction to make another wheel (cell, via complex chemical codes etc..). Then and only then is it possible to have two wheels (or two cells). So saying that life just happened spontaneously without the D.N.A codes for life in the first place is nonsense! So life was made in a completed state to start with, because otherwise neither cells or D.N.A could ever be made.

If the biological 'factory' (D.N.A) was not made to function on its own in a complete state to start with we would simply not exist. There has to be a chain of command to enable the materials we are made up of to combine together in ultimate complexity and order to begin with! In other words **life cannot just happen - it is made to happen!** How can cells form together if there is no way to make cells and no information or 'blue print' (D.N.A) to work from to enable the construction of life that needs to be uniform, well planned, timed right and sound in terms of structure, geometry, and much more?

Evolution says that life appeared from nothing and made itself over time! How can D.N.A construct and build itself? For life to change and get better the D.N.A code must be altered, and in turn written even more complexly and to a higher degree of brilliance, which simply cannot just happen. How can biological 'materials' decide what needs to be made and what alterations have to be carried out? The construction of life takes skill, superior knowledge, understanding and much more besides.

Matter can't think for itself! So saying life just happens is very narrow-minded and utter nonsense. The truth is cells are biological 'machines' that carry out the huge instruction code of D.N.A via extremely complex chemical reactions and sequences etc.. thus cells are brought together to form life but they themselves do no create! How can something that has no mind no artistic ability no intelligence, create anything? **It's just like saying bricks themselves build a house!**

Each building block in a person's body (cell) has D.N.A in it so each cell can grow from this massive and complex instruction code. We are made up of billions and billions of cells, all of which are linked to D.N.A.

By now you should be able to see the concept I'm getting at, which is that cells do not multiply and aid the construct life by chance! Of course not! They are instructed to combine together in certain formations which in turn are precisely executed in extremely mind-bending, complex and calculated ways, to form a creation of life from the instruction code of D.N.A - which cannot be made by chance either.......obviously! These things have been designed to function this way! They have been created to perform specific tasks by a creator of **immense intelligence**.

D.N.A makes life, because D.N.A is a fully-automated and ultimately well-designed biological building 'machine'.

Evolution makes no sense at all. It teaches that life makes itself, that life finds a way! This is quite simply impossible........**this is what is called a square wheel!**

Scientists look at the materials used in D.N.A i.e. acids, sugars, proteins and much more and record how they all react together and form life, but they totally ignore the incredible layout and design that enables them to work that way.

For example D.N.A is all laid out in order and when activated it starts to unwind, releasing the chemical codes of each of its parts; thus all the processes begin to happen which is mind-shatteringly complex. It is all quite simply the works of genius, someone who's understanding and knowledge is awesome. This display of creative power is the most impressive thing on in the universe; no other object or man-made construction can compare at all to nature.

When D.N.A is activated by fertilization of the cell many, many things begin to happen which are not understood. There is so much to learn about how we are made! If I started to list all the process and parts involved in this incredible design it would be enormous, in fact absolutely gigantic, and even then it would not be complete by any means.

So our D.N.A is made up of chromosomes (they determine what sex we are) which house gene codes that hold information about our individual features. D.N.A is designed to construct a 3 dimensional person, obviously, which again makes it even more complex. These codes are still trying to be mapped out and 'cracked' as it were today, using the most powerful computers in the world. The facts are, the information is enormous and many people all over the world can't help but admire the awesome crafts-manship, utter skill, engineering and technical understanding in such a thing. Yet they don't acknowledge a **creator.**

If you went into a top quality art gallery that exhibited paintings and sculptures, would you, after much viewing say to yourself? "I believe that no one created those."

Don't you think that sounds like a square wheel? Well if you think the same of D.N.A which is much, much, much greater in creative works, then you believe exactly the same thing but to a far higher degree of stupidity and foolishness.

Looking at a masterpiece by a great and talented artist, yet believing no one created it - that it 'created' itself is totally potty!

In Charles Darwin's day (one of the founders of evolution), scientists originally thought the living cell was a very simple organism that has a nucleus (centre) and some liquid around it, inside a membrane. Since then, scientists have discovered that cells are composed of hundreds of parts and have thousands of functions. They are still very far from understanding the incredible structure and functioning mechanisms of the cell. Today we know that there is no such thing as a simple cell. Now we understand that a bacterium is far more complex than anything built by man and the biological world is extremely complex and well organized. There is no laboratory on earth that can replicate the biochemical activity happening in even the smallest living organisms. The more we learn, the more we realize that it is beyond our capacity to understand in detail the dynamic chemical organization of the simplest cells. It is vital to understand that the cell is not just a blob of stuff that grows into life any old how! The cell and it's functions are more complex than computers. Cells are not just chemicals! It is like saying a book is just letters and not reading into it.

The cell is a complex system that has it's own 'power plants' that generate the cell's energy; 'factories' that produce proteins; complex 'transportation systems' that guide specific chemicals from place to place. The cell membrane acts as a 'decision-maker' as to what should enter and leave the cell. The nucleus acts as the central genetic 'government' and maintains the order for these processes. It also stores the 'blueprints' necessary for reproduction, D.N.A.

One of the tricks evolutionists can use to try to make evolution sound believable is to simplify the complexity of single-celled organisms, to make it sound reasonable to assume they could have appeared spontaneously.

Unfortunately some people can also overlook the complexity and design of these things on the basis of size. In other words if it is so small they think it can't be that complex.

D.N.A is not just some random mixture of chemicals that happened to form human beings over time. But rather it is an incredible structure which has been made so well it cannot be fully understood. Let there be no mistake about it, D.N.A and cells are not just a bunch of chemicals thrown together but rather the most creative 'sculpture' in the entire universe. People say there are Seven Wonders of the World yet they can miss the greatest wonder of them all i.e. nature, all life and the human body! We are incredibly and wonderfully made yet so dismissed as a work of creation! This should not be so. It is an extremely narrow-minded way of looking at life.

Scientists who believe in evolution don't really like to call D.N.A an instruction code (which is exactly what it is) because that means it was written. Remember D.N.A is like a software program for a computer that enables the computer to function by itself (automated). In other words D.N.A is the program or software and the cell is like the computer or hardware. But D.N.A is tremendously more complex and sophisticated than any computer program and the cell is still being understood today. Ultimately D.N.A has been written by a far greater amount of complexity and creativity than anything made by men because in turn D.N.A makes human beings, and we are the most complex and well-made things on earth. So all this creative power points to a supernatural knowledge and understanding.

D.N.A has been designed to work by itself, for instance when a mother conceives, nine months later she has a baby. All the incredible complex growth and structure of a baby and much more has already been thought out. This clearly shows immense creative power, yet it can be taken for granted. People can say that having a baby is a miracle but yet they don't acknowledge a creator. This is because people believe that life happens of its own accord. This is what evolution teaches i.e. that life makes and selects itself! But because nature has been designed to function in its own incredible way they think nature itself is the creator. Nature is a display of creative power not a display of nature's creative power. Don't be fooled by scientists who don't believe in creation, they're biased and want to look like they hold the secrets to the universe. Their theories are being read from the 'wrong book' which is not only the 'wrong language' but upside down and back to front as well!

As all things physical are made from elements found on earth such as iron, water etc, people think that a random combination of these materials made life. So let's study this purely material interpretation of nature and D.N.A's origins. To begin with we must understand here that for this to happen it must first be **possible** for it to happen. Remember that the elements are not alive.........of course. They have no intelligence - how then can they make anything? What insanity. It's completely daft! Yet so-called scholars and 'wise' people of this world fail to see this!! This simple fact is something that anyone can see. It's like saying that next time you go to a D.I.Y shop, buy the materials go home throw them in the garden and wait for them to do your D.I.Y for you! In other words a Does It Itself shop. If you're paying for a building job, pay only for the materials not the labour as it will be done automatically! Nature will find a way in time. What rubbish!

If you left a pile of bricks for let's say a billion years would you get a house?........No! It's that simple.

If you brought a mechano or lego set and shook the pieces

around in the box would it get made?...........No! Of course not.

Even if you got an extremely simple lego set and did the same thing you would have nothing! **There cannot be a probability of impossibility**.

For instance if you 'said' to a computer "What is the probability of throwing a dice and coming up with six, every time, non-stop for one hundred years?"

It would give you a number, but of course what it can't grasp is that it is totally impossible! Probability is mathematical and just numbers, but common sense is human and realistic. How can numbers be common sense? In other words you can give impossible things numerical values and a computer will calculate those numbers but it does not mean it is in any way possible...simple! Remember that mathematics is just numbers it's not common sense.

The trouble with scientists is they have no real grasp of common sense in their theories for evolution and the Big Bang (another evolutionistic theory) and if their mathematics gives them an answer they think it supports their theories......No! All they are doing is calculating the odds of something occurring which really cannot happen in the first place. It's rather like trying to calculate the odds of the number 51 ball coming out in the lottery results. The calculations you use to do this may be pretty good but no matter how long you wait the number 51 ball will never come out because there are only 50 balls. So **common sense rules over all calculations**. Impossible theories are given a 'probability' by numerical values. Then these values are worked out on computers and calculators that just pump out numbers and don't understand a thing. You can't give evolution odds of happening because it is totally impossible! A computer cannot understand such a thing! So don't be fooled by any so-called statistics that appear to 'support' evolution or the Big Bang. They are absolute rubbish!

Look at it this way: a D.N.A strand is very small but very complex. It is full of information or 'data' in chemical codes that are all squashed up in incredible inner space. If you took a tiny, tiny amount of that data, enlarged it and stretched it out, it would be huge. So let's say we have a piece a mile long. Now imagine that mile long piece as a giant game of Tetris even though D.N.A is far, far more complex. Imagine each tiny part which makes up D.N.A as one Tetris block and you have to fit them all together perfectly. The first block comes whizzing down, then another then another. It is common sense to say that it would never be completed without someone at the controls using skill and understanding. Otherwise it would become a complete mess with no utilization of space and no order. Like this the theory of evolution claims that all life with all it's incredible and complex D.N.A structures with absolute order just happened. This is a massive misinterpretation which needs correcting. D.N.A which is found in all life is like a completed Tetris game and in each case it is perfectly finished and fitted together soundly. This has been achieved by skill, wisdom and understanding....of course. In other words D.N.A is created. We are all part of creation.

Another point is many people allow themselves to be lead by their imaginations. For example if I said "Imagine a pool of goo."

It would be easy to do. Now if I said "Imagine a figure to rise up from that goo and become a man."

You would also be able to imagine that, some more clearly than others but it is easy to do. This is a real danger if you start to add the origins of human life to it because people start to base their beliefs via their imagination's and their understanding and wisdom is not guided by true knowledge that makes sense. In other words people's imaginations make up for what they don't understand and they add into the equation things that do not exist that have no common sense. People ultimately imagine that evolution can happen. Many people don't even understand the basics of evolution even though it is totally untrue. In other words they don't really care whether they understand it or not anyway! As long as it does not put restrictions on their lives and lets them live how they want and sounds 'plausible' they will take it in. Other people have been brought up with evolutionist theories and a high standard of academic education and are proud of what they know, yet because they don't want to admit they are completely wrong and swallow their pride they continue to support this theory. But rather than admit intellectual defeat they desperately try to preach evolution instead! Ultimately they are so proud they hate to be told they are wrong.....well you're wrong!

Evolution cannot happen, regardless of how much time is available; one thousand or one billion years. Even an infinite amount of time cannot make the impossible possible. A tornado could rumble through a junkyard for billions of years and would still not be able to assemble a bicycle which is obviously nowhere near as complex and well-designed as a human being!

Imagine a conveyer belt carrying bricks down it, and at the end of the track it dumps them all into a huge canyon. If you let that happen for however long you wanted you would never end up with a house, would you? The only thing that could do such a work is skill, design, knowledge and wisdom! This is logical. Life is made by a creator, not by the building blocks!

The human body is like a super giant jigsaw puzzle, and each cell being like a single complex piece. In this jigsaw there are billions upon billions of billions of pieces, in fact 30 trillion and it's not just 2 Dimensional but 3 Dimensional! Not only that but think of all the workings of the body including the brain which alone has 12 billion cells, from which there is more than 120 trillion connections! In decimal form that is 120,000,000,000,000. Just think of the understanding, skill and engineering needed to build the brains 120 trillion connections in complete order to function. The brain has 120 trillion connections and all are in complete mind-bending complex order and dynamic structure. Now if all the bits were shaken about for as long as you wanted, would you get a finished article? ....No! Of course you wouldn't. If the trillions pieces were repeatedly thrown in the air and back down on the floor you would get nothing but a mess. Even if some of it was built and you did the same thing you would end up with nothing but a mess...of course its common sense! Yet people believe that we were made from this random nonsense!! Evolution, like this imaginary jigsaw puzzle, does not have all the bits to even start with, but teaches that each piece has somehow appeared and all the bits make up this beautiful picture of life i.e. a human being. Now is that stupid or what?! And to top the lot some scientist somewhere would tell you there is a probability of the jigsaw being made! Err......no I don't think so!!

We are so very, very complex but all that complexity is in complete order! In other words you could say a giant plate of spaghetti is structurally very complex, but there is no order to it at all except random mess! But we on the other hand and all life are ingeniously designed to a great magnitude. Our bodies are designed so well and all the parts of our bodies are tailor-made to a perfect fit. Our whole physical structure is incredible. We are made up from complex varieties of cells which are in turn made up complexly of molecules that are made up of atoms, which are made of protons, neutrons and electrons which are made up of.....etc.......etc!!

In one drop of water there are roughly a million, million billion atoms! Just think how complex we are! We are made up of so many parts and all are works of genius! What a 'jigsaw puzzle!'

You must realize that thinking we just happened is what people are being lead to believe by the stupidity of others and themselves! The only thing that can make a 'jigsaw' like this is supernatural knowledge and wisdom. It's not hard to grasp that human beings and all things are the works of a creator.

Imagine a young child has a box of stickle bricks, which he then empties onto the floor, and cries out "I want you to build me a house!"

What would you reply? Would you say: A. "Keep on picking up the bricks and throwing them onto the floor and you will end up with a great house!"

Or B: "I'll come and make you a house if you are good!"

Now I think you will have to agree that reply B was normal and the reply A was insane. So why do people believe A. It's exactly the same as believing in nothing or evolution. As human beings are immeasurably more complex than a stickle brick house. I can honestly say that many children have more sense than so-called adults.

Thinking that we came from nothing is totally loony. It's just like taking a cartoon seriously. For instance we have all seen cartoons that show ridiculous events happening and it makes us laugh because of the stupidity of these things. For example, a house blows up and all the pieces fly in the air, then all the bits drop down and make another house even better than the first one. People laugh at these kinds of things yet they believe them in all seriousness when they subscribe to evolution! Can you believe it! What foolishness!

Belief in evolution is like saying that if you left a snooker table set up with all the balls laid out for millions of years, they would eventually go into the pockets in order with the black last! That nature would find a way! It's that idiotic. It's just total nonsense. A game of snooker is simple compared to the inner activity of cells, let alone the activities in the construction of a human being. But on the other hand if a professional snooker player used his skill, timing and precision, the balls would be potted i.e. creator. There are so many every day examples that show the stupidity of evolutionary ideas, yet still evolution is believed by many.

Saying that life makes itself or that life finds a way is like saying an ant wrote Einstein's theory of relativity or that an ant can understand a book on chemistry or physics.

Imagine a simple bottle with a screw top cap. Now imagine this bottle was buried on some distant planet in space and that it was discovered by men and brought back to earth. It would be on the news all over the world that this object was found; scientists would say "Amazing! Beyond <u>all</u> doubt this is the work of intelligence! Just look at its design. It's an incredible discovery!"

The public, scientists and the media would flock from all around the world to see this object! And it would be all over the news! People would wonder who made it! Yet why are people not questioning who created us and all life in awesome complexity and total balance? Just think how amazing creation is! It is far, far beyond our understanding. We are still learning about how amazing creation is today!

As I previously explained life cannot make itself. How can a deadness or nothing come to life by itself, it can't it's dead! There has to be a life in the first place to create life, thus we have been created by intelligence. This is clearly shown in D.N.A which is supernaturally made, also look at all things on this planet and beyond which are awesome, yet scientists and people seem to ignore the fact that just like the fictional bottle story, we too have been created! It is plainly obvious!

Think about when you see a car: you don't think that it made itself! Of course not, rather you know it has been designed and thought out by skilled people and engineered, there is no doubt. So why do people fail to see this in creation, which is far, far, far more complex and better made. I mean look at a woman! And if you're a woman look at a man! It is so obvious that it stares you in the face every day!

The power with which man and woman have been made is awesome and is not something to be taken lightly. The creative power behind such works as this is <u>incredible.</u>

Without a woman there would be nothing to make a human egg cell. When a woman eats, that food is broken down in her body and complexly used in many ways to maintain it, the food is also used to generate a woman's reproductive cycle i.e. periods. All these processes are <u>extremely</u> well thought out. A woman has a pair of ovaries that produce eggs (cells) that are incredible in their design. Without women we would not have the foundation of reproduction. Not only that, look how well a women has been made to deal with child birth, their hips are round and their legs are thicker to cope with the weight and on top of this think about the awesome power that shaped sexuality. We have been designed to be attracted to one another just by looking at one another. Believe me the amount of knowledge it takes to do such a thing is incredible. This power of attraction causes us to sexually interact (intercourse) and this causes life to be made via the D.N.A of each person. So the other half of reproduction comes from man and the man triggers the growth of the cell (egg) by his sperm. This all shows that human beings, both male and female, were created by someone who has the power to do anything.

When a women is attracted to a man it is done by masculine qualities that are interpreted by sight in the woman's mind from the design and physique and stature of a man. When a man is attracted to a woman it is through feminine qualities that are also interpreted by sight in the man's mind from the design of physique, elegance and curvilinear geometry of a woman's body. In other words both man and woman have already built into their minds the geometrical and 'mathematical' understanding of the human body of a partner without being taught! Again this just shows that man and woman really were made and designed for each other.

You should be able to see that the design of ours bodies cannot just happen. This is totally impossible. We have been made by superior knowledge that is still being worked out today! But people brush creation to one side and come up with ridiculous theories like evolution! The trouble is scientists have made useful things in the world, but that's the trouble because if the public trusts them too much, it gets to the point where you can trust and not question, and assume someone is right when really they are wrong. Have you ever heard that people can miss the obvious? Well it's obviously happened here. You don't need to be amazingly clever to see that evolution does not work at all.

Think about it. What other excuse would people use to dismiss creation? So just like the square and round wheels viewed from a deceptive angle evolution appears to work, but really it could not be further from the truth.

So now you can see 100% and more that this <u>theory</u> is not true! Here are some more facts that again totally destroy this terribly lame excuse for the origins of life and shows how the plain evidence of creation is falsified.

1. Evolution states that life somehow happened over millions and millions of years. If so where are the bones of all these half formed (forming) creatures that have so-called existed? Why is it that every creature found is complete? Why is it not growing a new pair of legs or something?! Why are creatures of today not in an evolutionary state of growth? Answer: because evolution is a square wheel!! If evolution were true there would be billions and billions of skeletal forms and animals showing growth of new parts all over the earth. We would have evidence coming out of our literal ears! Also think how much the earth has boomed in population in the last 100 years let alone thousands or millions!! Yet there are dinosaur bones here and there. So the earth is nowhere near as old as evolutionary scientists claim, they just say that to try and make it fit into their evolutionary theory. Also the so-called missing link between man and ape is non- existent because evolution never happened and will never happen. The only place evolution can work and exist is in the mind of someone who believes in square wheels.

Many people have been and are being fooled and mislead by evolution, just because they are not weighing up the pro's and con's and thinking for themselves constructively and there are different reasons for each person, but that does not make it true.

2. Scientists hide evolution behind big figures like millions and billions of years because they know that it would be impossible for someone to conduct an experiment to show they are wrong, because who can conduct a experiment over all that time?

So people are almost forced to believe them. So what they have done is taken something which is impossible and then slapped a millions and billions of years tag on it, to try and make it sound more believable! Utter nonsense.

3. Evolution is physically not happening and cannot happen so therefore if you believe in evolution you have belief in something that is impossible which is said to be possible on the basis that you

cannot see it happening. How convenient (You can't get any more blinded than that!).

4. Scientists believe evolution takes a long time and that given the size of the universe there is a chance that evolution can occur. But how can something that is impossible happen, even if it is given time?.................. Simple, it can't, no matter how much time or space is in the equation. There can be no chance of something impossible happening!! Chance can only exist if it is possible!

No matter how far or deep in space you were, the same rules of physics and common sense would always apply i.e. things cannot appear from nothing for no physical reason, also for every action there is a positive and equal reaction, order and organization.

Albert Einstein and Isaac Newton both studied the structure of the universe and saw that there was no doubt that intelligence was behind it. Einstein's famous equation E=mc2 shows that even small things have a complex and absolute order.

5. What came first, the chicken or the egg? Anyone who cannot answer this question will not believe in creation because creation is the only answer you can give that makes sense. We have already shown evolution is untrue, and an egg has to be laid by a chicken so the chicken came first, which was created, full stop. Evolution is not even in the equation.

6. A cell itself carries D.N.A and is an incredible foundation from which life can start it's amazing formation from the instructions of D.N.A. Now for a cell to be made you must first have a creature or life which has its own D.N.A that has been written and instructed to enable the life form it becomes to be able to generate or ovulate cells of its own in order to carry its own D.N.A, which in turn will enable it to reproduce. So like the chicken and the egg you need a creature first to make the cell, then the cell via the instructions of D.N.A can form into another creature. So creatures or life are created to produce cells which form life. So life is designed to make life, and life was created by life. This can also be put this way: - even the most stupid person in the world will tell you that a

book does not write itself, it is written (Yet if you believe in evolution that's exactly what your saying). This concept is the same with D.N.A which cannot design or write itself either and is far, far more complex than any book(s) in the world. Even a virus which is one of smallest organisms to have a D.N.A code does a particular job and function without having to be taught or learn! All life displays these qualities. Take a bird for example. Without being taught it can build a nest, this is just one of the many, many, many examples that again show that intelligence and being put this intelligence or 'built- in knowledge' into life.

7. Evolutionists take creatures that look the same and then stick labels on, saying "These are related - one came from the other."

Then they interpret the rest from there and see what they want to see, which is simply not the truth. But the truth is that all these creatures are different varieties of creation, which display even more so that the complex incredible structures of life have been designed and built.

But evolutionists also try to wow people with their knowledge of chemicals and scientific facts, and because they can explain in a certain amount of detail the complex way D.N.A and cells etc function people can believe their non-creation biased view because they respect what they have been told by them. Just because someone knows the materials used to make a house or anything of that matter, does not mean it was not built. Simple. And as I said before when you see something well made you know it has been made by someone.

8. We can 'adapt', as such, to the environment we live only because our bodies have been designed to cope this way in certain conditions. Our bodies can only react as our D.N.A design allows. For example, if a person's arm was cut off they would not grow a new one because people are not designed that way. Also if you banged your head this would cause a lump and bruise to appear, because it has been **engineered** into our bodies to react this way. In many other ways we can produce chemicals in certain situations to 'adapt' or repair, so this process does not happen of its own accord

but is made possible through design to cope in certain situations. Also if someone is a weight trainer their body becomes muscular with training......obviously, this happens because are bodies have been designed to work this way. Our legs don't suddenly decide to get muscular on their own! Of course not! And this development does <u>not</u> affect our genes (D.N.A), thus our children are not born with big muscles. If the body is hurt and becomes cut, your blood will clot and coagulate and a scab will form there. If you use your hands for hard labour your skin will thicken. If you go out into the sun you get a tan. This is because we have been created this way! This is not evolution but good design.

9. Creation and all life are governed by laws of creation. This is clear to see. Science is making a terrible mistake. Remember big mistakes in history happen. Evolution is a **theory** based on impossible, warped and bent ideas. Let me ask you would you trust someone you didn't know with your child? If you believe in evolution then this is exactly what you are doing, trusting people you don't know with something very precious - your mind!

You could say you don't know me but the thing is evolution makes no sense, but what I say does. A person who tells the truth always makes sense. The trouble with evolution is the amount of broadcasting it receives globally. Many people are basing their judgement in this matter on the majority rather than truth. Many programmes on evolution look and sound impressive but saying it evolved makes no sense at all. Anyone who makes no sense in this matter is either confused of a liar.

So how creation works and functions can be studied and is science, but saying it built itself makes no sense, and is not scientific, just like saying a book writes itself. It really is that simple.

So here is a simple formula that underlines much complex and detailed truth.

Creation = sense
Evolution-based 'science' = nonsense

10. Evolution states that life gets better i.e. that life forms into

better creatures. But as explained evolution is impossible, so it can never improve. How can a small animal change into a human being?! Need I say more? Also life shows that D.N.A is getting worse i.e. more deformities and different kinds of illness etc. Some of this is due to radiation from nuclear reactors or other unnatural sources and harmful chemicals etc, although this is compensated for by medical research and better nutrition and quality of life. So D.N.A can be like a photocopy, i.e. if you keep on photocopying a copy its quality is reduced. This is a fact as we all know and it is the same in nature, and the whole universe, in scientific terms this is called the second law of thermodynamics or entropy, simple. In other words things go from order to disorder or complexity to decay. But scientists totally contradict themselves in evolutionary thinking by saying things go from decay to complexity and disorder to order. Imagine someone saying to you after you had written a huge essay and been given a F- for it "let me make a copy of that essay and then another copy of that copy, and I'll do this until it starts to fades, but don't worry the essay will be far better, perhaps worthy of an A+!"

I think you would have to agree that this person believes in square wheels!! But that is what evolutionists think about D.N.A, that ultimately the human race came from an 'F- organism' to an 'A+ organism' through millions of years of reproductive evolution. Perhaps in the future some time we will all grow wheels so we can get around quicker as the modern environment is very fast paced! Unfortunately they would be square!

So if you ever hear someone talking about the second law of thermodynamics or entropy you now know it is simply common sense that shows that things go from order to disorder, in other words natural decay.

11. Evolution is a <u>theory</u> that was thought up by men - one of those being Charles Darwin who at the time used very primitive science, it was in the mid 1800's that he came up with this ridiculous idea. So basically the foundation of evolution is old, primitive and thought up by men who's understanding of nature and biology was very limited. Darwin just took animals that had some similar features

and started grouping them together, hence evolution. He also observed that some creatures would hunt for food in different ways in a given environment. But so what? This proves nothing. Of course creatures will do different things in different environments to stay alive, but this does not mean they will change into human beings!

Remember people first thought the world was square, like a square wheel, and also flat. But now with proper understanding and logic we realize it is round, like a round wheel, and 3 dimensional. The same principle applies to evolution it can only 'exist' in the imagination it is not a fact. So over the year's people have been told about this theory which cannot work and ultimately used their own imaginations to make it 'work'. Hence over time science has got to know more about biology and nature and added evolution into the equation. 'Teachers' have become proud of their so-called 'knowledge' and become biased in teaching the theory of evolution. Thus as the world has moved on in terms of technology and telecommunications this theory has been commercialized and spread globally very fast and is constantly being used by a whole variety of media. It has got to the stage, like I mentioned before, where if many people accept something that is wrong, other people will not even question if it is true or not. It reminds me of some words said by a great man "A little bit of yeast makes the whole batch rise."

12. With the education curriculum influenced by scientists who believe in evolution, it is a stumbling block from day one for many youngsters and older students. Also many in-depth educational programmes have been made for television that support evolution, which are viewed by all age groups. Many people all over the world find animals and nature fascinating and like to hear how nature functions. Many documentaries have been well made and narrated on this subject, but only in terms of showing the way nature functions, not how nature has been created to function. Nature clearly displays a **divine intellect.** These programs push creation aside and try to link in evolution instead. So because evolution is linked to educational programmes and other study material people swallow it as well! People can take it in without realizing!! Evolution is so cunningly mixed in, that it becomes almost 'tasteless' as it were.

Think for instance about programmes on the human body. These all display creative power, and the programmes themselves are like beautiful cakes that are well decorated in terms of displaying the wonders of nature. Then just as it is time to put the cherry on top, a heavy brick is thrown down instead, which totally ruins this beautiful display of creative works. This is what happens when evolution is attempted to be linked in, it is just like having a nice cake and ruining it with destructive nonsense. But creation is the cherry which finishes it off perfectly, to enable a person to have their cake and eat it.

13. St Peter's church in Rome is a huge structure that's well built. It has beautiful carvings and designs all over it. Many people from all over the world go to see it. The building is a real feat of human engineering and design, but it does not come close to the design of the human body! Think how complex our minds are alone. There is nothing that can come close to the design of ourselves. It was man that made St Peters. So as I said before it is obvious that when something beautiful is made like St Peters, which consists of a high degree of order, skill, knowledge and understanding, it takes a far, far higher degree of these qualities to create a man or woman to build it in the first place! If something as good as St Peters was built by man, who made man? Who is behind the creation of the world?

14. Now think of another beautiful building, any one you like, as long as it is impressive, as this reflects nature and us. Imagine this building was left alone for 500 years - would it be looking worse or more beautiful? Of course it would be looking worse! Now imagine a thousand years have passed, what would you expect to see, a new extension built? Or perhaps an even more dynamic building? Now that is pure madness, but this is exactly the same principle that evolution uses – 'that things can naturally improve over time.' What rubbish. The simple fact is they don't. Evolution is **not** the natural law. Remember there can only be a one-in-a-million chance of something happening if it is possible in the first place! There is no chance of evolution happening – this is the natural law.

15. Part of the impossible lie used in evolution is a process known as natural selection. By which life 'became' through changes in its surrounding environment causing the fittest to survive. But what does that prove? Of course some creatures can survive different environments while others die – so what? Have you ever heard such clap trap? If I went out to a fish pond and pumped all the water out most of the creatures in it would die, of course. Maybe some small or microscopic creatures would survive, and that's it. It's the same principle if many creatures lived in a forest then there was a forest fire – some would die while other lived on. But this is what science calls a part of evolution! What utter madness. Natural selection is just an evolutionistic way to interpret a creature surviving an environmental circumstance. So the so-called evolutionary 'process' itself 'married' with natural selection is just a loony, insane, warped, bent, ridiculous and embarrassingly pathetic impossible lie. How does the 'natural selection process' re-design a creature to a greater level? Think how much intelligence is needed to re-design a car, let alone life on this planet! For instance if you took a single fertilized human egg (cell) which is about 100th size of a pin head and stored the D.N.A information from it into books, you would need all the libraries in the entire world!

After this non-existent 'natural selection' jargon also comes the totally backwards ramble of evolution by mutation!! That life gets better by becoming worse! Evolutionists actually think that genetic mutations are part of evolution! It's just lie after lie. Let's think about this - why is it called mutation? In other words deformity!! So really poor Joseph Carey Merrick (The Elephant Man) or the fictional Hunchback of Notre Dame had nothing to be concerned about, because according to evolutionary 'science' it is an improvement!! There is no such thing as evolution by mutation, only natural decay. Nature clearly shows that all life dies. Evolutionists are looking at life and interpreting any desperate excuse to try and fuel their lie. Mutation is a change that proves life is dying – going from order to disorder from complexity to decay.

It would be appropriate to point out that to get deformity you need perfection in the first place! This clearly proves all life was created in a perfect state to begin with.

So it is plain to see that genetic change is not evolution. Rather evolution is a false interpretation of change. There are changes that are possible and changes that are impossible – evolution is an impossible change.

We have been created to see things in sound terms of geometry, form, structure, colour, tone and 3d etc, so it is easy to know whether something is getting worse or getting better, it is in other words common sense. For example you could say that if someone was born with an extra eye this would allow them to see more, but it is plain obvious that it is a hideous deformity rather than improvement.

I can't get over how stupid evolution is. Do I really have to write these simple facts? Basic primary school intelligence has more sense than evolutionary 'science'.

16. Evolution teaches the survival of the fittest. This is what Hitler picked up from Darwin to reinforce his plan for the destruction of the Jews and the rise of the 'master' race (Germanic Aryans). He was totally against creation. Hitler took evolution to its ultimate pinnacle, which is death, destruction and utter hate etc. Herr P. Hoffman in his book Hitler's Personal Security, said "Hitler believed in struggle as a Darwinian principle of human life that forced every people to try to dominate all others; without struggle they would rot and perish...."

Carl Marx was another who picked up these insane ideas that are evolutionary based, in a book called 'Des Capital' which influenced the rise of other dictators like Mao Tse Tung and Joseph Stalin (Stalin was responsible for more murders than even Hitler according to current research in Russia).

So murder, genocide, hatred and violence are all part of evolution and survival of the fittest. This is why Hitler and those with his mind set have (had) no time for people with Downs Syndrome, those who are chronically ill, the elderly, the mentally retarded etc and are happy to exterminate (abortion) and experiment with humans in their mothers wombs for the sake of convenience, in the name of scientific research.

Yes abortion is also seeded from evolution, and tries to justify the murder of children by saying that when a child grows in the womb it shows the different stages of evolution that shaped past of mankind. This warped theory has got an over-the-top name that sounds impressive. This is common with scientists to label things with names that sound intellectual, the name is recapitulation. Recapitulation is obviously wrong but some believe it! Can you believe this madness?! The development of a child in the womb shows the incredible design and power of a creator, the knowledge and wisdom that has gone into the structure of a human being and the complex growth that happens in nine and a half months inside a woman is mind shattering. But of course hair brained evolutionists think it all just happens... yeah....yeah.....yeah.......boring....yawn, they can't even see past their noses.

So as a result abortion was conceived, and slowly began to poison the weak-minded to this day. One man in particular who fuelled this destructive fire was a Dr. Carl Sagan (evolutionist) who basically said that the killing of a human by abortion was like "The termination of a fish or frog."

Yeah right! That's how many evolutionists minds work. Anyway this madness provided the legal framework for abortion and is still used today. People who believe these kinds of teachings have no truthful structure in.

Here are some more facts that show abortion is murder plain and simple:

When someone is asleep are they still human and alive? Of course they are!

If a tree begins to grow is it not a growing tree? Of course it is!

Is a child of seven not a human because they have not grown up fully yet? Of course they're human!

Does age make a person expendable? Of course not.

17. 'Natural selection' as we know is non-existent and cannot explain how a creature with gills can become a creature with lungs. For instance. This impossible occurrence is said to take millions of years and happen in tiny stages, but gills and lungs are totally

different. So how would the creature survive with half developed lungs? And why would lungs be so-called forming over millions of years anyway if they are of no immediate advantage to the species?

Like I mentioned before life is made by the creator, not by the building blocks. Otherwise the theory is that this creature is dragging around a half-formed set of cumbersome lungs for so-called thousands or even millions of generations. There would, in this lame theory, have to be an immediate advantage for this change otherwise the 'natural selection' process involved would not continue to pursue the particular direction it has taken, especially over millions of years. So therefore if the creature is surviving without lungs, why should the need for lungs arise?

18. Centuries ago it was thought that insects and other small animals arose directly from spoiled food! This false, pathetic theory used to be called spontaneous generation. Many think society has come a long way since then, yet people believe the same ridiculous principle nowadays i.e. that life just happens! If you believe that life just happens please realize that you are allowing yourself to accept absolute nonsense. If you teach evolution can I just say that beyond an utter shadow of a doubt you are unfortunately deceiving yourself and others into accepting a teaching that has all the logic of a catapult with a stone tied to it or a chocolate fire guard or inflatable dart board and of course a square wheel!

19. During the world wars man began to build primitive computers, but during the second world war in particular the Germans used a code that allowed them to communicate. This code was scrambled up so it could not be read or understood. The code was called Enigma and the Germans made many Enigma machines to use the code. So the code needed to be unscrambled or 'cracked'. For a while the code could not be understood but eventually the code was worked out by the aid of a man called Alan Turning who was compelled by the notion of automated computers. So using skill and understanding and creative intuition he made a machine called the Bon machine. It unscrambled the code and started the already small but growing foundation for the computer age.

Another machine was built called Colossus and so on and so on. Now even before the first of any of these ideas, inventions and creative intuition is all life the human body and D.N.A which like the Bon machine is fully self automated and built and designed to a far higher and ingenious degree of creative power. It is obvious that even before man thought of computers that we are the works of creative skill and understanding, just like the computer machines themselves! And finding D.N.A just underlines that fact. Yet it is strange that the facts of creation are ignored by many!! People don't doubt whether computers have been made using creative understanding so why do many people doubt that life on this planet has been created? The simple machine made by Alan Turning was said to have been way ahead of it's time, yet look at the human body, brain and life itself!! This means that anyone who does not acknowledge God is a complete hypocrite, because they have lost touch with the plain understanding that we have been created. This obvious fact is all around us but it is not scrambled up like the enigma code but easy to understand yet people are scrambling it up themselves. Just like Alan Turning made the code-breaking machine, so God has put his 'machine' in us. In other words our minds see and understand the beauty of what is around us in nature and we can see that this is the work of creation. (Everyone can see this but it is either kept, ignored or thrown away.)

20. Fossilized remains of a creature known as a coelacanth (you might know the name) have been found next to fossilized dinosaur bones. Yet the coelacanth is still alive today. If evolution were true this creature would have started to evolve by now and why did it not become extinct? So how do evolutionists try to explain this away? I saw the answer to this question on television, the programme tried to suggest the coelacanth survived evolution! What a completely lame excuse! It's still the same today because as explained evolution can never happen and is like trying to add 2 and 2 to get five! There was also no solid explanation of why it did not become extinct. So now we not only have survival of the fittest but survival of evolution as well. How can a creature decide not to change or change for that matter? Need I say more?

The real reason why creatures of today are found fossilized next to extinct dinosaurs is explained in chapter 4 'Round wheel of truth'.

21. So the truth is simple about all creatures here today: they never evolved because evolution is a square wheel, which is utter mechanical nonsense. Evolution is a childish story for so-called adults.

Put it this way: in 1922, a single fossil tooth was discovered, which evolutionistic scientists interpreted in their, biased and warped ways to belong to a kind of monkey man! Now not only did they think that the impossible was possible by evolution but they were that desperate to rule God out and find something to try to enforce their stupid, senseless lie that they began to dream up an ape man creature from a **single tooth**. Most people think that the ape man concept is a fact. But it is not. The truth is so simple: there is no such thing as ape men. That is why you get the concept of the 'missing link'; in other words scientists are trying to find links in fossil records to prove evolution, which they are still doing today.

Anyway the single tooth thing went completely over the top and using a lot of square wheeled imagination the scientist's involved made up an ape man from this single tooth. Then the press got light of the story and by the time the story was released not only was there a painting of 'Nebraska man' but also a 'Nebraska woman'. So one tooth ended up being called Nebraska man and woman..................yeah, there's one word that sums this up..................Sad. By the way the 'discovery' of this mangy tooth happened just as the physician, Davidson Black was about to run out of money for his project and evolutionary explorations in 1927.

Anyway some time after the initial discovery, an identical tooth was found, by a man called Harold Cook. But this time round the tooth was artificially attached to a human skull, and then the skull was attached to the skeleton of a wild pig! Thus yet another 'Nebraska man'. Then they slapped a big name on it to make it sound over people's heads and intellectual thus it was known in 'scientific' terms as Hesperopithecus haroldcookii. They must have been thinking if no one can pronounce or read it they won't ask questions about it. Again...sad. This so-called discovery went on to be shown as a fake just like evolution is today. But unfortunately, like people today, it was believed to be true. But that did not stop the evolutionists.......oh no. They then went on to form another monkey man, this time claiming he walked upright. Again this was given another intellectual sounding name, Pithecanthropus Erectus and termed Homo Erectus and has the nickname Java man.

Guess what? All this from an incomplete skull (just a bit of the cap) a leg bone and three teeth. On top of this madness the leg bone was found fifty feet away from the skull bit and a full year later.

Then after all this insanity yet another monkey man arrived called Piltdown man. This time round the father (as it were) of evolution, Charles Darwin was involved. Piltdown man was actually the jaw of an ape stained to make it appear as though it matched a human skull, the accompanying bones (not a full skeleton but just bones) were stained and reshaped also some of the teeth had been filed down to look pointed and different.

All the scientists of that time approved of its 'authenticity' even though it was crudely faked, including of course Charles Darwin.

It wasn't until around forty years later that it was found to be a complete fake, and in all that time it was used to con students and many other people into believing evolution was true.

Again nowadays there is another so-called true skeletal form that tries to explain evolution, the name of this 'skeleton' is Lucy. Its basic parts put together, to try to build a lie! This nonsense is labeled in the evolutionary world as 'The ape that got lucky'. I'm sorry, but when I heard this I had to laugh! What fools!! These people are so blind that they think certain animals (if not all) in time will get a human brain and if they 'want' human legs as well they will get them!!.......So on and so on.........yawn, yawn boring!

It really is terrible to see people committing intellectual suicide by actually thinking up and believing such <u>total refuse</u>, to put it mildly! What's more, some of the people involved in useless projects like this actually believe their findings are true!

Palaeontologists put things together in such a way as to counterfeit evolution. Let me explain: when you buy a jigsaw puzzle you first look at the picture on the front of the box, then if you like it you buy the puzzle. Then when you get home you start to build the puzzle from the picture. Evolutionists do the same thing, in principle, with bits and pieces of fossils but unlike the jigsaw puzzle they have no truthful picture to work from, only their interpretation of that picture. So they put parts together to fit their own picture and make pieces 'fit' that don't match the facts. When they build some skeletal forms they use their understanding of skeletal structures but also their misinterpretation of the picture to build a lie. For example - in the past there must have been many species of apes and other animals, which have not yet been discovered, that had different shaped skulls and skeletons just like there is today. These creatures would have become extinct, and some of them are uncovered bit by bit, thus evolutionists think they have found missing links in the so-called 'chain of evolution'. Other parts of these extinct creatures are put together to create animals that try to 'support' evolution. These people build and interpret things in this way because they are foolishly pretending to themselves and others that evolution is true, yet it is so obvious it is false! You must realize that ape men are <u>fictional</u>. There just bits and pieces put together to counterfeit and interpret a complete lie. These bits and pieces are few and far between. Pay no attention to images of 'ape men'. They are simply derived from people who are so sad that they think they are related to animals! They are just making monkeys of themselves.

22. Here is another point to think about: As you were reading this book you would have learned something, and that information is now in your mind. The reason it is in your mind is because the brain has been designed to store information and understand things. This process is incredibly complex, our brains our structured in perfect order and dynamic function. i.e. one part of the brain does one thing and another part another thing, and the whole system of the brain is all linked up together.

So learning is just that 'learning', nothing else. The reason I'm writing this is because there are people who think that learning is a form of evolution! For example scientists have and still are carrying out experiments on monkeys to try to get them to understand speech and many other learning tasks. Yes, they are being paid to try to get monkeys to learn and then claim it is evolution!! When human beings talk and understand things it is because we have the 'hardware' to do so. A monkey cannot do such things like a human being as their brains have simply not been created with the same 'hardware'. In fact because animals don't learn and understand on a human level they have been created to be born with built-in knowledge about bringing up young and many other things and all that comes from the creator!! Don't think that a monkey has an undeveloped human brain that is total lie. A child has an undeveloped brain of course, and it's not the learning that makes it grow, it's the D.N.A coding that makes this happen. So a child learns because it has been made to learn and understand, and as the brain grows to full size it allows us to understand more. Obviously, the more you study the more you will remember and learn. This is not evolution but rather shows the incredible design of the brain. The brain is rather like the muscles on the body, they can get bigger, stronger and more powerful with use and get weaker smaller and less powerful with little use, but their basic structure from D. N. A does not change at all. Development is not evolution. Could an ant learn complex speech? No of course not, because it does not have the 'hardware' to do so.....this is very simple knowledge. In this respect an ant is the same as a monkey – it cannot change! It can become a little smarter, as the design of its brain allows but that's it. It's exactly the same for all animals, a fish, bird, reptile, mammal etc, etc. Think of understanding as a computer programme and the brain as the computer. Now if you made one programme and put it in the computer so it was 'smart', would the hardware change to a more sophisticated machine on its own? Again another example, if you had a computer that was not powerful enough to run some complex software, would the computer upgrade itself? Of course it wouldn't! How can it know how to upgrade, it's total nonsense!

So our brains store and collect information simply because we have been designed that way! Learning itself is a part of creation - we were designed to learn. For example look at babies and young children: it is natural for them to learn and be inquisitive. The fact that children and babies learn makes them very sweet indeed. Also learning is dependent to certain degrees on the personality of the person and teaching of the individual. In other words if you are educated and taught a lot you will know a lot and if you are educated little you will know little. This is not evolution but common sense. If you teach a dog to lie down it will not change into a horse! (Anyway it's not really how much you know it's whether what you know is true or not.)

23. Evolution is taking the creator's beautiful, wonderful, lovely and knowledgeable works and ruining them by throwing him out of the picture! Remember the capacity to learn is from the capability and extreme complex design of the brain, and this structure is made through D.N.A. which was in turn made by a creator. One of the problems is if a person does not know the seriousness of this issue they will ignore it. But really how can you ignore who you are? Think seriously about how well-made we are. It is plainly obvious that wisdom and knowledge have made us.

Believing in evolution is more stupid than trying to walk through a wall, when common sense says 'use the door'. As not only do we have the obvious and plain knowledge that a creator has made all things, but we also have the knowledge that has just been explained above, and much more. Please try to re-educate yourself if you don't believe in a creator. It is not tough, wise, cool or intelligent to ignore these issues.

D.N.A in truthful principle it stands for **Divine Natural Architecture**. That is what D.N.A is: the most well-designed, complex and brilliant code in the world.

Think of a frog: It begins as frog spawn: thousands of tiny clear balls with back dots in, then after some time you get tad-poles then they grow legs etc...etc....until they are frogs. That is an amazing process that happens in all living things. All evolutionists have done is looked at the same thing and said, it needed legs so it got some, or it needed arms so it made some. Or nature itself give it legs, by causing it to change in its environment.................Somehow I don't think so!

24. Here is another point about A. I. or artificial intelligence. Some evolutionists think that making computers is part of evolution!

These people are very, very mixed up. They think that creating sophisticated machines is evolution? What? Err? Hey? I think it must have something to do with the film 2001 Space Odyssey where human evolution is depicted, and man goes to space and is accompanied by a computer called H.A.L. who goes berserk. This sci-fi film just feeds the imagination! As explained evolution is impossible and building computers shows the abilities given man to learn and understand things.

The human mind is far, far, far, better built than any computer, I mean a computer is just semiconductor switches and high and low voltages. Computers come nowhere near to processing or duplicating the complex feedback, physical grasp, approximating and assessing functions, but to name a fraction, of human thought! Evolutionists are thinking backwards. As for the late Arthur C. Clarke - how mistaken he was! People like him think they are so intelligent that they become proud and stubborn.

25. Babies and children have been designed to have facial characteristics that combine together to give a kind of sweet, lovely, cute, innocent attractiveness that is interpreted in our brains automatically! This is sheer genius. For instance many people can have their caricature done by an artist. This of course takes skill and understanding. When the artist draws what he is really doing is exercising the incredible ability we have to feel a certain way through shape and form. You will notice that if a person is drawn by a caricaturist they almost always end up 'baby-fied' as it were, i.e. large forehead and small squashed up face. This same principle is at work in the animals too. They have been designed to portray certain visual qualities that stimulate the mind. All this is creator's design.

Also when we have certain feelings our faces change to show that particular emotion, this again is absolute genius. If someone looks at us in an angry way we immediately know a threat, we see this through complex visual interpretation of our minds. For example when a baby is born they can cry and automatically know how to screw up their face and attract attention. When a baby is happy they can laugh even though they were not taught to do so, they show many other different displays of emotion and facial expression. This again shows amazing creative power.

If what I'm saying was a lie then why does it make sense? Simply because it's true! I'm writing this book to open up people's minds to the truth of this world, which people are failing to see. So don't ignore creation, rather acknowledge it. Remember these obvious works are self-evident, it's no fairy tale. Creative power is all around us everyday. You can't see the creator directly but you can see his works, it is so simple. Does this seem too good to be true? Well, it is true. Also remember that everything that is man-made has really been set in motion by this immense creative power. Who do you think gave man the mind and physical ability to do these things - the creator of course!

Don't be fooled by evolutionistic scientists who have got government funding and so-called understanding. They know nothing but ridiculous **theories** that are broadcast so much that people can take them as so-called fact.

If you believe in evolution you may as well say that anything can happen, and be unsure about virtually everything! Because that's the foundation that your laying. People actually believe they came from a heap of goo at the bottom of a swamp at some point in time and that they are related to animals! Do you really want to believe this? No wonder people can suffer from things like depression and can feel lost, thus people are slowly crushed by the apparent meaninglessness of life, and also society begins to break down because people follow their instincts, so there is no real right or wrong, no sound guide and no real accountability.

However the sound guide we should all follow, that shows what is right and wrong, is explained in chapter 4 'Round wheel of truth'.

Ding......................Next!

Chapter 3

The Big Bang (The Big Lie).

At this present time people seem to believe that the world was made by a mysterious Big Bang of energy and basically using some 'maths' and square wheeled theories this made the earth, sun and the whole universe, for life to exist on a delicate balance. Not forgetting that after this impossible 'occurrence' comes yet another impossibility that we so-called evolved to become human beings.

Now let's think about these points. For starters the calculations used by scientists and mathematicians to wow people with the Big Bang are based on **theories** that exist only in the imagination, that have in turn come from warped ideas. Basic primary school intelligence tells me that explosions do not create - they destroy! No matter what! If you take a match and light the end of a banger or fire cracker it will explode of course, and it will destroy itself, because that is the nature of a bang. So basically a bang 'kills itself'. How can someone even start to say an event like this makes anything, other than a complete mess? Also it takes order to make a bang. For example bombs are thought out and designed then after this they are destroyed. So please remember that even to start off with the Big Bang <u>theory</u> is backwards!

The bigger the bang the more chaos and randomness is in it, not order. Chaos is the most unstable and destructive equation of them all and people believe we came from this? What absolute and utter garbage. Let me put it this way: some people can laugh at the chances of winning the lottery, yet they believe in the Big Bang! How can chaos and randomness create? Let's think about it: what is chaos and randomness? What are their principles? Chaos is exactly that, **chaos**. In other words no order, no sense, non-creative, not thought out, not logical, not meaningful.

Think of a blank canvas and a bowl of fruit, ask an artist to paint them as realistically as possible and you will find that their actions to paint them would not be non-sensical, meaningless, ill-logical, disorderly or non-creative! NO of course not! Sense and logic would be behind every brush stroke. Thought would go into it. Why then do people believe that this whole universe came from chaos and randomness which is impossible and complete lunacy!!

In the whole universe there is an abundant amount of organization. This abundance is overwhelming. It is all around us in all things also chemical and atomic structures, the amount of information is numerically mind-boggling, just the information in a single human cell is incredible. This has all come about and been put into place by immense knowledge and understanding, not an explosion.

Chaos and randomness are by-products of order and organization: first comes order then chaos i.e. to make an explosion you first need to make the bomb itself, which takes skill and understanding and knowledge. It is like this with the stars: they themselves are designed to function a certain way through hydrogen and helium to make energy and light, so therefore the sub-atomic structure of the molecules inside hydrogen and helium are designed to act in a certain way to make this happen. Why do solids, liquids and gases form under pressure? Again this is design because without them you would not have life! Who made the elements to function the way they do? The periodic table shows that elements have been made in a particular way. Why do certain elements have a certain amount of protons, neutrons and electrons? If you asked scientists why the periodic table is structured this way they would have to admit that elements are like they are in order that they can be used as building blocks for life. This shows that the elements themselves have been designed to design, rather like bricks for a house.

So how can a Big Bang - that cannot happen to start with - then go on to make the elements that in turn would be needed to make it in the first place? This clearly shows the Big Bang is a Big Lie.

The Big Bang <u>theory</u> is reverse science, yet it claims to be scientific. Why do people believe such fantasy? How can people who believe in the Big Bang say they are clever if they think the world was made by an explosion? If the world was made by destruction, then there should be miracles happening all over the world that are due to absolute chaos and disorder, like in Hiroshima when the atomic bomb went off: people should have been healed from sickness and small forms of life should have been 'created'. The Big Bang is also a Big Excuse. I hope you can now see just some of the disturbing lunacy in the Big Bang theory. I would say that the only way I could believe in the Big Bang were if my real name was indeed Rumple Stilt skin. The only way something like the earth could be made was if it were made by someone. Someone with intelligence made the world because only intelligence could think up such an amazing universe; so complex, well structured and dynamically balanced in its existence. Nature shows the nature of someone, that's why it is called nature. Things are divinely or supernaturally made, they simply did not just happen by the complete chaos and destruction of an explosion.

There is another **theory** derived from the Big Bang theory itself called singularity, which of course is total garbage. This states that the universe can be compressed and squashed down so much that it basically becomes single, and this so-called true calculation is supposed to back up the Big Bang theory - that from single point the universe popped into existence! Oh how convenient! Just like a kids pop-up book! It is true that matter can be compressed into a very small space, but so......what does that prove?...............Nothing! Any calculations beyond matter being compressed into a small space are purely theoretical. The only thing that is in any way truthful about this singularity <u>theory</u> is the single brain cell used to think it up. Something has to be made in the fist place in order to be squashed up anyway, so apart from being totally wrong it's backwards, upside down and inside out. People who come up with <u>theoretical</u> excuses like this try to use phrases, words and calculations that get people confused, in the hope they will get lost in the explanation but believe what there taught on the basis that scientists know things they don't. Also a lot of the time some people who preach rubbish-based <u>theories</u> like this can deep down resent belief in creation. Maybe because they are bitter in some way. Basically when they use their mathematical calculations they count things that aren't there.

The origins of the universe can never be found and are untraceable because the physical world was not made by the physical but by the unseen. Some scientists are trying to find out how we got here by sending out satellites and performing space exploration but it's like trying to think of a new primary colour: you simply can't do it, no matter how clever you are.

Also don't be confused by people who go on about the birth and death life cycle of stars. For example as I have stated nature clearly shows that life dies. This includes stars they can implode or explode sometimes as supernova. When this happens scientists think that the aftermath is new life as it were......rather like saying if you burnt something up the ash and smoke from it are its re-birth......err no. Science simply can't admit that the whole universe is subject to decay it is not developing but dying.

How can something physical happen from nothing? There has to be a cause that is not physical. Tell me one thing that happens that does not have a cause?........There simply isn't. The cause for the whole physical world and the universe is a creator who exists in a different realm.

There is also another delusion that is reflective of the Big Bang and evolution, and this is atheism. An atheist is someone who believes in nothing at all - that everything just came from nothing!.........Sound familiar? People who believe in nothing believe in the same principles as people who believe in the Big Bang and evolution i.e. that nothingness made everything and everything just happened. What utter, square wheeled nonsense and complete gibberish.

So as you can now see evolution and the Big Bang are just theories that make no sense when viewed properly from angles of truth. Also believing in nothing is to accept that every thing just happened which is what evolution and the Big Bang state.

People could say to me "You are not a scientist."

And I would say "With theories as stupid as the Big Bang and evolution I really don't want to be. If that's what people think is clever count me out!"

Evolution is the **Evil Solution.** The Big Bang really is just a **Big Lie.** A lot of evolutionistic people who teach these things have their engines running but there is no-one at the wheel. Their theories on the existence of human life are based on ego and pride, not evidence. They just want to look clever to their fellow men and the public. Instead they try to make certain parts of these theories fit in with mathematical equations and try to blind people and themselves with science. I'm glad I don't believe my relatives are ultimately baboons. The Big Bang and evolution go together hand-in-hand and boil down to 'the same belief' which makes no real mathematical or scientific sense, they're just child's theories that hide behind very, very, very long periods of time. Which means in other words 'excuses for the unknown'... But really the origins of the universe and life are not unknown, they are all recorded and plainly accounted for. This is what we will explore in the next chapter - 'Round wheel of truth.'

Chapter 4

Round wheel of truth.

This is the truth, which works soundly just like a round wheel. It explains how all life and the universe came to be without any complex maths and stupid theories: what I am saying is that someone made the world, not some 'event' - **God** is the one who made the universe and all things, he has clearly made his presence known in the things he has created. This fact can be plainly seen by what is in nature and by human beings. Look at the sun: it shines on the world in a perfect balance, not too hot not too cold. Look at the moon that gives light at night. Look at the stars that can be used for reference of times. Look at all the rainbow colours in nature and the design of trees and plants. See the beauty of water which makes the seas, rivers lakes and ponds. Look at the bedding's of grass stretched out like a carpet over the land. See the blue sky with its magnificent clouds. Smell the flowers and enjoy the incredible variety and beautiful designs of them. Also enjoy tasting and eating an enormous selection of fruits and many other foods. Look at the incredible design of the body. Think about human feelings and emotions. Look at the designs and faces of animals. Think of the huge variety of animals! See the beauty of children and the way they make you smile. Think about the miracle of childbirth and the way a child grows to be adult. This overwhelming display of natural architecture shows the works of a creator which cannot be denied. The belief that God exists is not some long-lost tale, but it is clearly evident to this day: God's power and divine nature are perceived in the things God has made. Creation has acted as a constant 'advertisement' for God from the first day of mankind all the way through history to this present day.

The reference God has used to keep man to his sound guide that was recorded from the time of God's creation, is the Bible. Think about it what else would he use?...........A computer?...Of course not.

This book was set into operation to keep Mans' connection to God, it's very simple. The Bible explains all about creation and the origin of our existence on earth. So it is vital for mankind to read the Bible to see what the truth is, which God reveals.

So creation shows a fundamental truth in it which is that God made all things, but there is something wrong with nature that is evident in the whole of creation. What do you think it is? Answer: everything that lives dies. This is the ultimate destiny for life on this planet. In fact everything in the whole universe whether it is biological or material is subject to decay. So why is this? What is the explanation for this?

What we need is a reference that can tell us who it was that created us and the whole universe. We also need an explanation as to why everything that has been created dies. Now for starters the Bible explains all this in the only way it could be explained, which is in truth. It says that God is eternal: he existed and exists eternally. He is not physical but spiritual i.e. unseen, he made two realms, the physical and spiritual. In the physical realm he made the earth and the whole universe and all life including us, the human race, both male and female. In the spiritual realm he made a domain for spiritual powers and authorities i.e. angelic beings (angels). Their function besides other things is to interact and govern the principles and structure of the human race by means of spiritual interaction that is unseen. In other words they would govern our actions to a certain degree without us being aware of it in totality.........does this seem hard to believe?........Think about it, look at the beautiful design of a human being, look at the structure of all things. We don't question if a well-engineered car has been made by men? So why question God's works which are far, far, far better engineered and made?.........So believing in the angels is no big deal at all, the same power that made us made them, simple.

So we were made by God who in turn made the earth to provide us with fruits and grain as food. When we go shopping we can walk past all the fruits and grain items and not even give them a second thought. Yet that food is picked from trees and plants that God made to start with. He gave us a wonderful variety of flavours, colours and shapes that all are uniquely different. This is not a fairy tale rather it is a powerful truth that is being ignored by a large number of people!

In the Bible it says that God made humanity male and female. That's why we are called man and woman. This comes from the Bible: the earth was created in six days and God rested on the seventh to mark it as holy. That is why we have a seven day week. It is also why we rest on the seventh day (it is often called the day of rest). This again is all Biblical and plays a huge part in our lives!

Also the fact that we use the stars as a guide for times of the year comes from the Bible. We also use the moon as a time reference i.e. months, but God also placed it there to help women calculate period cycles and to give a delicate glow of light at night by reflecting the suns light. The Bible also explains many, many other so-called mysteries of our existence that have all been Biblically accounted for from the time of creation. But without going into too much detail you can see that what I'm writing is pure, plain and obvious truth.

The Biblical account of our race at the time of creation was two people, male and female. At that time we did not understand the difference between what is good and what is bad. The names of these two people were Adam (male) and Eve (female). They both lived in a part of the world called Eden where God also made a beautiful garden grow called 'the garden of Eden'. Adam and his wife were both naked but they did not realize they were thus they could not be embarrassed. This is all recorded in the first book of the Bible, Genesis, which means origin.

So at the time of creation death did not rule over the world. The earth's whole eco system was biologically different in many ways. Animals fed on vegetation not on each other and human beings lived in a perfectly balanced world. But the Bible explains the human race was ultimately cursed with death by God because Eve was tricked and tempted (by an angel who turned against God) into disobeying a powerful commandment God gave to human beings. Adam also sinned against God by doing what Eve (his wife) did. They both ate fruit from a particular tree (which stood in the middle of the garden of Eden) which God told them not to eat from or even touch. But in doing so they were given the capacity to understand what is good from what is bad. The tree they ate from was called 'the tree of knowledge' as anyone who ate from it would become wise. This event is not just some story or fairy tale. It actually happened and has altered the existence of the whole course of the world and the universe. It is the very thing that answers the question about the death of all life on this planet and the decay of the universe.

If you think about it, only a God who is evil would make a creation only in order for it to die. So there has to be a valid and accounted reason as to why and how death spread into a perfectly balanced world. The answer for this is clear for all to see in God's reference book and sound guide for mankind, the Bible. It states that one of the most powerful spiritual rulers i.e. an angelic being (angel) whom God created to do certain spiritual works started to think about his own greatness in comparison to God's. He ultimately became jealous of God. He became proud and wanted to become higher than God himself. In this proud state he started a rebellion against God, based on principles of evil. Thinking that his plan of rule was fail-safe he managed to convince about one third of God's angels to follow his rebellion as he was greatly admired as an example of perfect conduct and wise intellect in the spiritual world (until he became evil). This angel's name was Lucifer and at some point around creation he deceived humans to disobey God, hence we were cursed with death.

This event is the most altering in history. It happened exactly as described in the Bible: we were tricked by lies and temptation (via a snake whom Lucifer entered, giving it the power of speech) to eat from a particular tree that God had directly commanded Adam not to eat from, or any other human being. The fruit from this tree would enable us to become wise opening up certain 'pathways' in our minds. Giving us (as previously written) the capacity to decipher what is good from what is bad. This change of interpretation in our minds through understanding would be carried into our offspring. By God's power our D.N.A would have been altered, also with it God would have changed our biology i.e. D.N.A to be subject to decay and death. Not only that, the whole eco-system would have been altered and animals would have at some point started to feed on each other, the harmonious balance of a perfect a peaceful creation would now be subject to death, hardship and pain.

This would have all happened on a molecular level and initially would have not been self-evident. The only thing that was self-evident as stated in the Bible is the awareness of being naked. The Bible says that we became aware of our nakedness when we were disobedient and ate from the tree of knowledge, then we were given understanding. Think about this point: why is it that we wear clothes apart from it being cold? What other reference describes this and explains why? The Bible even explains embarrassment, so the very fact that we get up in the morning and put clothes on shows the direct connection to this event. Everyone knows that deep down they understand about the modesty of the human body and know without being taught about nakedness. This is why we sometimes blush and become embarrassed because we were born with that understanding, which as stated shows the reality of Genesis....obviously.

The account of Adam and Eve from the Bible states this event happened somewhere in the Middle East near four rivers which divided from one stream (Genesis 2: 10-14). This fact is still evident today, also in this part of the world many precious stones are found there. Also think about this point: you came from your parents...obviously, and they came from their parents and in turn they from their parents, so if you went back in history eventually you would get to the point where only two people exist....again obvious! These two people are Adam and Eve...very, very simple, but a very important fact. (Recently it has been discovered that all people came from two human beings)

But before we move on there's another point which needs

answering. Can you think what it is? Answer: we came from two people, so why do we have different races? This is the natural question to ask, and of course the Bible answers this perfectly. So let's look into the reason why we have different races in the world today (so as now explained God is real and this has to be addressed, anything else is a <u>square wheel</u>).

Apart from many other events after creation and the mistake of mankind through deception, the world obviously started to grow in population, and in those times peoples' mind set were more focused on God but there was still a great deal of ignorance and rebellion. Men began to work to their own devices and please themselves so they started to build a city and built a tower called the tower of Babel (Genesis 11: 2-9). This tower they built in defiance against God. (By the way the oldest dated man made structure is <u>less than</u> 6,000 years old, this fact fits in with the Bible, the truth of course.) But as stated God saw that they were wrong and in his great understanding knew that he had to divide them up in order to stop them from all going against him. So he made them all start to speak in different languages instantly and they divided up in panic and wandered off in groups confused by one another. God also changed their genetic characteristics in order to create a visual divide. Again this would have been done on a molecular level and not been immediately self-evident, apart from the change in language. So God changed their D.N.A structure, hence different races of people so these qualities were introduced at this stage to stop a <u>total rebellion</u>, amongst other reasons.

God gave some people very dark skin to cope with the sun and hot conditions. To others he gave very complex language etc...etc. (Note: language is decreasing in complexity, newer ones are more simple than older ones - this totally contradicts evolution).

This division of the world is another major event in earth's history that totally changed the course of humanity, and is of <u>vital importance</u>. It should not be overlooked.

There is now another question that needs to be answered from what has just been explained: it is a bit deeper but makes natural and constructive sense to ask it......can you think what it is?........It is to do with the part I wrote about on the characteristics that God gave in order to cope with the sun and very hot conditions......?

The question is this: How can the earth be subject to hot conditions as it was created perfect? And as stated after our mistake through deception the only changes that took place as far as you could see were on a molecular level, so what other event could make the perfect world become too hot and have major variations in temperature and climate.....etc because that is how the world is today........so how is this explained? If the world was made perfect how come we have summer and winter, hot and cold? These questions are not hard to answer if you use the truth as a guide. It's like looking for a place using a sound map...no problem. The sound map you use is the truth 'God's reference and sound guide the Bible'.

The answer to these questions and much more besides are in Genesis again. The Bible states that the world started to grow in population but before the tower of Babel's time people acted the same way and defied God and his rule ultimately to please themselves (Genesis 6: 5-12). God saw how wrong they all were, so in his great understanding he sent a huge flood to cover the whole earth that would wipe out virtually all living things.

But one man and his family tried to do what is good so God gave him instructions to build an ark i.e. a big cargo-like ship. On it he took many pairs of animals male and female and his family, no one else got on the boat although they were warned about the flood by this man. The man's name was Noah, many people are familiar with this event, but they fail to take it seriously. Not taking this event seriously is a very big mistake, as it stops you from properly understanding about the earth's truthful history. We must remember again that creation is plain to see, and God's command can bring into existence what did not exist, so sending the flood is no big deal at all.

Anyway I'll briefly explain why we have summer and winter, but later on I'll explain in more detail this item and other implications that lead from it.

At the time of the flood the earth was completely covered by water and it was very stormy. Massive forces of pressure and water circulation would have destroyed everything on the earth's surface. Also due to this enormous amount of water the earth itself was under a huge strain caused by the increase in its gravitational pull. Another contributing factor was the moon's gravitational pull which would have drawn a huge body of this water to one place. So as the earth rotated it would have started to spin off its normal axis. As this was happening huge volumes of water would have started to freeze at the poles causing even more imbalance. Then to put it briefly the whole earth tilted on its axis wobbling slightly and the crust of the earth cracked and fractured, due to the huge forces acting on it. That's why as stated in the Bible when Noah finally occupied the earth after the flood, God said to him you will now have seasons, summer and winter (Genesis 8: 22).

That's why to this day we have four seasons, spring, summer, autumn, winter. The fact that the earth is tilted on its axis is the reason why we have seasons. This factor could not be properly understood by man until fairly recent times when man started to explore space and the planets. Also as I mentioned the earth's crust fractured and cracked. That's why we have earthquakes through history. They all occur down or near massive fault lines in the earth's crust. For instance the San Andreas fault line in America runs straight through the major cities, God has purposely made it that way. These massive fault lines outline giant continent-sized pieces of the earth's crust called tectonic plates which are constantly shifting against one another causing earthquakes. There are about sixteen in all. So the very 'foundation' of earthquakes was set into motion by God through the flood. Evolutionistic scientists think they know about the earth's history but they're just dealing with the symptoms of creation's fall and the flood, which were caused by God's judgement.

During the flood the cracking and movement of the earth's crust under this massive amount of water caused some of the newly formed tectonic plates to buckle which produced certain mountain ranges in the world. The earth's crust sits on top of molten rock called magma which is very hot, and in certain parts of the world the movement between the plates or cracks during the flood would have caused the magma to rush out. This would have acted like underwater volcanoes of today which solidify quickly because of the water it is immediately exposed to. This is why today we have volcanic islands and other volcanic related masses around the earth.

Many people miss the fact that the flood really happened, but it is totally obvious that it did. If you go into your garden or virtually anywhere you will find pebbles. Don't you usually find them at the beach?.......So why are they all over the place? Answer: again the flood. These pebbles were made by water smashing and crushing stone together under enormous pressures. However, many beautiful stones (pebbles) were made at the time of creation, just as they appear today.

The tell-tale marks of the flood are evident to this day i.e. some extremely high peaks on the earth have great caverns in that were once underwater, and these caverns have swirling marks ground into them by rocks, stone and other material. Some scientists don't know how they got there, because they are against the Bible. Instead they try desperately to find ridiculous <u>theories</u> to dismiss the Bible, but the simple fact is this was caused by the flood. Also many other marvellous sights around the world of strange natural formations are all linked to water and global flooding.

This major event totally explains in depth and complete truth why many of earth's creatures that were made at the time of creation by God were wiped out in a flash. These creatures' remains were first discovered in the late 1700's and they went on to be called the dinosaurs. Again here are the end trails of the floods massive damage and destruction which again is falsified.

There are huge mistakes and 'square wheels' in the evolutionistic version of the story of the dinosaurs, although the study and excavation of fossils is interesting. But the so-called facts relating the dinosaurs are wrong. For starters, evolution can't happen as totally explained (can you believe some scientists actually think T-rex, one of the biggest and carnivores dinosaurs, is so-called related to a bird because it skeletal form looks similar!). Mind you they think they came from baboons! And in turn from some goo! So anything goes with them. Put it this way: I think I would like a DVD player so I'll go and take my old VHS player and plant it in the garden. I'm sure that nature will find a way!

Anyway as I just mentioned the evolutionistic layout of the explanation of the disappearance of the dinosaurs is wrong. To begin with they did not live 360 million years ago. For instance fossils are not old, they just look that way. I'll explain: bones are made to be lightweight yet strong, so if you examine a bone you will see under a microscope that it is full of holes. There are other reasons for this but this is basically how a bone is made up. So when an animal dies its body degrades and the skeletal form is left. So if the skeleton was covered in sediment, i.e. liquid thick mud with concrete-like substances found in the earth, this would prepare it for the process of fossilization. Now just one other ingredient is needed.........and that is tremendous pressure. Now as we all know, if you go swimming and dive down to the bottom of the pool you can start to feel the water pressure, so imagine how much pressure would be in say a global flood, the water would be miles high. This in turn would cause the sediment to go into the tiny holes in the bone thus forming a fossil....simple. This is not some silly theory but is a fact. Today in certain parts of the world they find just this, at the bottom of very deep water sites they find fossils of everyday creatures that recently died. So fossilization can occur under pressure and the right conditions in a very short space of time.

So don't be confused when it comes to fossils, because they are not a great mystery. They are made in conditions of tremendous pressure, exactly the same conditions described in the Bible when the earth was totally flooded. Many fossils can have not just the bone fossilized but also the flesh! Which shows they were fossilized in an 'instant' (ammonites can be found with the tentacles fossilized). This fossilization occurs by the creature getting encased in mud etc then as the pressure builds up around it, caused by the enormous volume of water the sediment around the creature begins to solidify, then as this happens the flesh itself rots away and a cavity is left (small hole in the impression of the flesh). As the pressure increases the cavity gets filled with minerals...etc that solidify making the fossil. This fossilization of flesh process has only happened with the smaller creatures, because the flood lasted forty days and forty nights, then started to go down, so only the creatures with little flesh would have been able to fully rot away making the perfect cavity.

Ammonites are small creatures that lived on the continental

shelf (shallow water around land) and as I have just mentioned some are found with the tentacles fossilized, but also these creatures have shells and when you examine the fossil you will find a shell in the fossil. Many other fossils of creatures like this have the actual shells and some are so clear that if you rub them with your fingers you can see the 'mother of pearl' effect on the shell.

Also in certain parts of the world they have actually found dinosaur fins and skins that have been discovered by big fishing vessels, many from the shores of Japan. Again in the polar ice caps they have discovered thousands of mammoths, even baby mammoths, some are frozen solid in the ice and well preserved. Many people have used the ivory form them for different purposes.

The New Siberian Islands (north of the Siberian Arctic mainland) have yielded an abundance of fossils (mammoth, woolly rhinos, musk ox, antelope, horse, deer, bear and more than 50 other species) requiring forests and meadows to sustain them. Embedded in Arctic muck are a large number of mammals that have been frozen before they could start to decay. In Alaska, duck-billed dinosaurs, turtles, conifers, herbaceous vegetation, and broad-leaved trees bear testimony to a tropical environment that once existed (just as the Bible describes, at the time of creation).

A U.S. Geological Survey Report submitted evidence of tropical vegetation in Alaska: mangrove, palm trees, Burmese laquer trees and others. In 1998 a champosaur, an extinct subtropical crocodilian, and turtles were discovered in the Queen Elizabeth Islands in arctic Canada. Obviously such a reptilian was not mobile enough to migrate. This would require a temperature range of 25° to 35° for an area that currently sees temperatures of -45° degrees!

A similar 'lost world' is frozen in place at the South Pole. The geologist, Peter Barret, was one of the first to look for fossils in Antarctica. He discovered an amphibian jaw belonging to a creature that could only have survived in a warm, damp environment. This gave rise to many questions so various palaeontologists followed his lead. Thirteen thousand feet up Mt. Kirkpatrick in Antarctica (around 400 miles from the Pole) pterosaurs, carnivorous theropods, and many other creatures have been found. All this evidence begs the obvious question "How could animals like dinosaurs, flying reptiles, and turtles survive alongside ferns and conifers in areas with very low temperature and months of darkness?"

So obviously, there was once a dramatically different climate at the poles. The discovery of thousands of well-preserved leaves in Antarctica has also sparked a debate among geologists (evolutionists). This all shows that these animals and plants were subject to a global flood which came upon the earth very quickly. It also shows the earth's climates changed due to it tilting on axis.

Look at crocodiles and alligators: they are reptilian like many dinosaurs and the only reason they are still here today is because they did not die during the flood or naturally become extinct over time. God made many large reptilian creatures at the time of creation that were destroyed in the flood, so saying the dinosaurs are pre-historic is nonsense because all creatures were created in six days as recorded in the Bible.

Also because the earth tilted on its axis many species of plants that existed before the flood, which flourished in a good environment, became extinct because they were not able to germinate and re-grow in the new change of environment caused by the catastrophic effects of this event. That's why certain types of vegetation are fossilized and others are labeled 'pre-historic' too. The simple fact is they were all made at the same time. So don't be fooled by any scientists who claim the earth is millions and millions of years old - date labels like: Jurassic and ice age are not existent. It's just scientists wrongly interpreting the earth's history caused by the flood.

Before we move on I'd just like to bring something up out of the blue to catch anyone off-guard. It goes like this; some people actually believe that God 'made' things through evolution! Now that has to be one of the most stupid ideas going, apart from the theory of evolution itself. How can evolution, which does not work at all, be used to make creation? Creation is created! It is totally backwards, upside down and inside out. It is not only a square wheel but a flat one as well! Anyone who thinks this is unfortunately very mistaken indeed!

So let's just go over the points about a global flood but with more information added, to get an even stronger and well-established picture.

So at the time of the flood the whole earth was covered with water. This event destroyed much vegetation, animals and all human beings apart from Noah and his family who were aboard the Ark. Many creatures which did not board the Ark became fossilized during this time. The Ark was filled with land animals and birds of all kinds, in order that they should re-produce again once the flood had ended. Also the axis of the earth changed when the flood reached its maximum. This was due to a number of different factors that God set in motion i.e. the gravitational pull of the moon and sun on the flooded earth and freezing at the poles, all attributed to cause the whole earth to tilt on its axis. (Just in case you did not know the moon and the sun's gravity is what gives us tides of the sea, and waves etc.) Albert Einstein made a hypothesis about the earth tilting on its axis and he calculated that this would be possible due to imbalance of weight at the poles! So this just <u>adds</u> to the reality and truth of what I'm saying. Enormous amounts of new water would have started to freeze around the poles as it began to tilt on axis, thus causing even more instability as the earth rotated. Also huge bodies of 'old' ice that became subject to a different temperature as the earth began to tilt would have broken from their place.

At the time of the flood I strongly suspect that the earth was hit by a comet(s). This comet(s) <u>could</u> have come from one giant comet that broke up as it approached the earth (roche distance) just like the Schumaker Levy 9 meteor fragments that hit Jupiter in 1994. But one thing is for sure, there are a few big and obvious impact sites around the globe to this day. One of the impact sites is in the area that is now called the Yucatan Peninsula, in the Gulf of Mexico. This huge comet would have hit the earth and caused insatiability to the earth's crust, and would have blackened the sky greatly around the impact site with huge amounts of dust, thus causing strange weather conditions in a very short period of time. This could have been part of God's judgement on the world at the time of the flood (to fracture the perfectly-created structure of the earth).

The comet(s) would have partly fractured the earth's crust, so that when the flood was in 'full swing' the earth's crust would crack, as it tilted on axis. The impact(s) would have also helped to release the vast body of water that was under the earth at that time (Genesis 7: 11-13). When the world was first created this water would come up from beneath the surface and water the ground all around the earth.

There are roughly three major impact sites around the globe that can fit into this picture. There is one in Mexico, Canada and India. The marks of such big meteors and comets are still evident today. The crater left by the impact strike in the Gulf of Mexico is 120 miles wide. The crater is known as chicxulub, and the body that made it has been estimated to be as big as Washington D. C.

Comets like this would have affected the earth greatly (especially if there was more than one impact around the same time). Huge amounts of dust etc caused by such an impact(s) would have been thrown into the air at great speed. The dust would have covered enormous areas, but as the flood gained in force the rain would have washed some of it down and it would have soaked into the ground. Huge amounts of this dust would have been carried in the water of the flood and been dispersed over much of the globe. I suspect this explains why to this day there is a thin iridium layer (rare heavy metal) that is found in many places around the world in the layers of earth.

The comet(s) that I suspect God sent would not have been directed to the Middle East because this would have destroyed the people living around that area and of course Noah and his family.

Before the flood the earth was more tropical in its climate and conditions. It was 'watered' by underground springs and a fine mist like dew, which relates to much better or perfect conditions, this adds to the reality of the perfect world the Bible depicts. Maybe it would have rained very gently with small droplets every so often. But it only rained heavily during the days of the flood. There was also a 'dome' of water vapour that lay in the upper atmosphere (Thermosphere) that gave the new created world the perfect conditions, which was to be destroyed and spoiled due to Mans' separation from God (Genesis 1: 6-8). The Bible also states that the land on the earth at the time of creation was together in one place and the sea was around it (Genesis 1: 9-11). But after the flood all that changed. So sending a huge comet or comets seems plausible to God's plan and judgement, to fracture the earth's surface allowing huge volumes of water to come up from below the earth quickly. These fractures were the first stages in the splitting of the earth's crust, creating tectonic plates, that today cause earth quakes.

So as the water began to rain down heavily on the people who were living at that time they would have then known there was going to be a flood, which they were warned about by Noah. As the rain got heavier the sky got darker, then lightening and thunder began. In certain parts of the world living creatures would have been covered in mud and sediment. The flood lasted 40 days and nights and in that time there would have been massive amounts of carnage and destruction.

Then the water pressure would have increased more and more and caused fossilization and other things as previously explained. Plants and debris would have been made into the fossil fuels of today. That is why they are called fossil fuels, like oil and natural gas. Scientists can make fuels of this kind in laboratories using the same kind of conditions in less than 20 minutes. Much of this matter over long periods of time would have been eaten by bacteria and to this day we get many underground areas of gases that can bubble to the surface in the oceans that contain methane gas. Thus a lot of carbon is put into the atmosphere. This of course is turned into a square wheel by scientists who don't link the Bible into nature simply because they are stubborn, wrong and biased because of pride.

Anyway the water from the flood got deeper and deeper and eventually covered the whole earth, creating enormous pressure (Genesis 7: 18-21). This and other circumstances put into force by God caused the earth to tilt on its axis and the earth's crust to crack, causing all kinds of formations and volcanic masses on the surface etc........as explained. Also the earth's temperature and climates would have changed dramatically. After the 40 days and nights the flood stopped and the water started to go down. It would have taken a long time to go down completely and would have gone down in stages in certain parts of the world, thus creating marks and patterns in sedimentary rocks and mountains that to this day are explained falsely. Some of these markings are exactly horizontal which shows that water made them, yet they are far higher than sea level. The Bible states that the boat with Noah, his family and all he animals came to rest on a mountain range as the waters went down. From there they all went out of the boat onto the land.

After the flood man was told by God to repopulate the earth. Also God set a sign in the sky to show he would never completely destroy the earth again with a flood and that sign is a rainbow. That is why we have rainbows today and they are linked to water and the flood because a rainbow is caused by the action of light on droplets of water (God has made it that way). So a rainbow directly shows God's promise (Genesis 9: 8-17).

A rainbow has seven colours and God is stated in the Bible to have seven spirits that make up himself, this is why the number seven is related to the Bible and God. It's why we have a seven day week, and when God made the earth he rested on the seventh. God himself obviously does not have to rest but this was done to set an example to mankind to mark this as his holy day, the seventh day. This is also why people think the number seven brings good luck, which is nonsense. Seven is obviously just a number, but it represents God, who is very real. Again there can only be one truth and the Bible is it. Nothing else fully explains about how death came to be in creation and how it all fits together in a perfect uniform picture that makes dynamic, structural sense. It's like looking at a sound building: you can tell if it is sound by analyzing it and looking at it, reading the signs, in the same way the Bible is right by looking and reading.......simple......if you don't look, you don't see.

But some people simply don't want to acknowledge any truth about God because deep down they don't like the thought of a superior authority, and would rather live their lives pleasing themselves. Also many people know that the Bible teaches good qualities like love, kindness, understanding, humility, patience, morality, gentleness and has laws on sexual conduct which does not suit them and their life styles so they like to dismiss it and claim to be unaware and oblivious to it. Yet God's creative power is plain to see.

People can find it 'easy' to dismiss God because he is unseen, or exchange the truth about him for a lie, for the sake of pride and human nature's convenience.

Many people prefer to be totally indifferent to what the Bible teaches is right and can be rude, slanderous, loud, violent, fierce, selfish, immoral, perverse, lustful, ignorant and have no patience or tolerance for others, show no kindness, be unthinking, unkind, liars, 'drinkers' and much more besides. People can be 'drunk' on the feeling of power, pleasure, superiority and pride they get from being this way. Many actually think they are clever to live like this and that they are good. This could not be further from the truth.

The trouble is that if many people act in these ways others learn by their example so it goes on and on getting worse. Plus some people who accept the Bibles teachings can get caught up in behaving in this way too and can fall away from what is right.

It is foolish to actually think this is the right way to live but the simple, plain truth is that this way of living is totally wrong, and is a 'by product' of the non-creation belief in the world. The people who died in the flood shared he same mentality as this. If there's a lesson to be obtained from the global catastrophe of the flood: it's to acknowledge God by keeping in mind the sheer obviousness of creation and living a life which he considers good. But to believe in God truly a person must have faith in Jesus Christ which is explained in Chapter 7 'Tracks of truth left by the round wheel'.

Chapter 5

Trimming off any square corners.

So now you can see a much clearer picture that has come about by thinking constructively and using <u>common sense</u>. There is much more information that all points to the Bible, some of which we'll go over later. But it's not just the knowledge and wisdom from the Bible which explains and fits into everything perfectly, that can start to convince people about God, but it's how you let that knowledge into your life. Let me explain: for example, someone can be told about these facts, but then forget them quickly, or people can hear the message but not listen and take it in. If your attitude is wrong the words of the Bible can't settle in and grow properly in the mind. You see, when you accept the Bible you let it into your life, as it were, in 'two parts': one part is the acceptance of its knowledge and the other is the acceptance of the way it teaches you to live and behave, which as I previously wrote, clashes with human nature, so in turn people know about creation and other dynamic teachings of the Bible but are cunningly pushing them into a dark corner due to ignorance and other human desires. Thus they are failing to acknowledge what God has made plain about creation. This ignorance is carried through generations and people throw out the most important knowledge of all.

For example, why do we get married? This is from the Bible. Why do we use the word divorce? Again from the Bible, and much of the structure of our language has strong Biblical reference, for instance.......Good (God), evil (devil), bad, sin, woman, man, day, night, light, darkness, lie, truth, gospel and <u>so much more</u>. These words all go back in history when the Bible was being translated from the original Hebrew version, which originates from the Middle East. In England much of the translation of the Bible was done in a small town in the Midlands, England, called Lutterworth, which is evident if you visit there. Also think about how much the Bible is interwoven in society in terms of Mans' architecture, think of all the old and new churches around the world. Think about Sunday schools and the impact the Bible has had on schools and other places of education. Also think about the impact it has had on some political issues globally. The Bible also teaches how and where the gospel spread when it was first preached and as we all know this has to do with Jerusalem and the surrounding areas, also Rome in Italy and all around that area. That is why there is so much Biblical architecture making up beautiful buildings of all kinds, this clearly shows the impact it had in these areas and the way in which the message of the Bible spread, moving up into Europe and reaching out everywhere. This fits the Bible's account of where the message of God and Christ was first spread and founded. So the whole world can clearly see the reality of the Bible's influence throughout history to this present day. All this information is well-known knowledge, but many put it aside, and allow themselves to be consumed by other things and fail to see the reality of it.

We can have very busy lives, and may have to work hard, but this does not mean that creation and the Bible's teachings are expendable or unrealistic views on life. The variety and stunning beauty in creation is enormous; the designs of everything are always on display and constantly advertised, all of which show God's existence, but missing this fact gives a person's life no real meaning and can cause people to think that nothing really matters. Nature is a display of many things, one of which is the fact that God can do all things. Missing God is like denying your own reflection in a mirror. You would have to be a fool to do this, but God's 'reflection' is in nature, 'staring' back at everyone. It is undeniable, yet it is ignored by many.

People today can be well aware of the many increases in wrong-doing and other indecent things that agree with human nature, which are against God, but they do not try to understand what is truly good and what is truly bad. This is because they simply do not read the Bible, from which all morality, goodness and truth is based, as God made all things and set everything in its place. The Bible's instruction is like a lamp that shines in a dark room that shows the truthful lay-out of the room, but without that light nothing can be seen. Living life without the Bible's instruction is really like walking in darkness, which makes no dynamic sense, like the square wheel.

Sometimes we can receive too much information from everyday life, so people can throw many issues and questions on the 'back burner' and not search through everything to see what the truth really is. So before you know it many peoples' thinking becomes sloppy, muddled, confused and unfocused on the truth from God. If someone receives many different types of opinionated information faster than they can weigh up the pro's and con's, they miss out great chunks of information that is vital to know, and in turn they can let things into their mind they haven't thought through. This is one of the big problems with television, and many other condensed and compressed information media. These highly influential media that are in the world affect everyone. The human mind has been designed and created to work around a certain pace, so too much information too quick is unhealthy especially if all the information is mixed with powerful images. For example television is always reporting and showing trouble in the Middle East, and many power-ful images of violence. Many people relate all this trouble directly to the Bible, (as it is around this area of the world that many Biblical events took place) then they go on to say religion causes wars. But in reality the full teachings of the Bible in both old and new testaments together are not being fully accepted by many in the Middle East, thus this adds to all the trouble. Not only that but there are other religions all around this area and much fighting and war which has nothing to do with what the Bible teaches is right. So television can give a false 'square wheeled' angle on what the truth really is, so the truthful information people need to hear is lost in the confusion of television and other media like it. What makes this worse is that many people are also too subject to the way human nature interprets issues. So due to a lot of confusion people can say that religion causes wars, and they would be right as long as they meant that <u>wrong religions</u> do. Let me put it this way: the Bible teaches not to kill, to forgive, to live in love and show respect towards one another. It also teaches to hate wrongdoing and to try to get others to believe in God's extraordinary saving grace and love, through the death of his son Jesus Christ. The Bible teaches what is good, right, proper, pure and correct. Other religions when studied and examined have many 'loose ends' and do not make total dynamic sense. They can also serve to give the truthful religion of the Bible a bad name by their violence and needless trouble. Thus many can ignore the truth and consider it evil. It's like a school class full of pupils who are all messing around and being disobedient, acting loudly, violently and foolishly. All apart from one pupil who is standing at the back trying to make peace and order, but he is drowned out and ignored. Then the class is punished for their behavior but no exception is made for the one good pupil who did the right thing, so he also is punished with the others. But if this case had been examined more closely it would have been found that he was not to blame and should have received praise for his good actions. This is exactly what people do to God's teachings through Jesus Christ when they consider them wrong because of the image of religion in society. A religion that is a lie will inevitably cause trouble and needless pain. Also the Bible teaches what is right - it's people who do what is wrong. It is men who sent out troops to war, not God.

So not only can television 'pump' information very quickly into large numbers of people through opinions, but also powerful images. Images have very powerful effects on the mind. Sexuality can be powerful this way, in influencing people to behave in ways that are opposed to which the Bible teaches. Because sexuality can be so powerful in many corrupt ways, it can make people biased and stubborn toward the Bible, to the point where they can become very angry and very anti-religious because they love the way in which they are being led by human nature.

Television and other media all around the world are mostly controlled by people who don't believe in God and Jesus Christ, thus a huge amount of information is broadcast into peoples' homes which ultimately has nothing to do with God and 'drowns out' his message. The trouble is the media in this world are all based on making money so people are told anything that suits their human nature in order to sell or get high ratings, which in turn makes money. Human nature likes gossip and things that are obscene which fuel lustful desires and other human attributes and so do many people who control television. So the whole thing has spiraled into an ungodly, mixed-up mess that can really damage and confuse peoples' thoughts.

So here are some more points and facts I have collectively written to enable people to filter out any more lies and confusion which television and other media can cause. So remember what has been written previously. Take it in at your own pace and it is a good thing to re-read this information so it can settle.

It must be remembered clearly and firmly that evolution is non-existent, as it hinders so many peoples' thoughts. So another point to underline is that the earth according to the truth, (the Bible) is around 6,000 years old. I have already gone over some points that show this is true but here are some more:

The rotation of the earth, which is currently about 1000 mph (1600 km/h) at the equator, is gradually slowing down. The reason for this is the gravitational drag of nearby celestial bodies, such as the sun, moon and other contributing factors. If the earth were billions of years old, it would have already stopped turning. Going back, 5 billion years ago our planet would have been spinning so fast, it would have been shaped like a flat pancake. Obviously the earth is not billions of years old.

As the earth's rotation is slowing down, the moon is gradually receding from earth. This fact has been observed since 1754. By measuring the speed of the recession and the moon's distance from earth, we find that the earth-moon system cannot be old. Just 20-30,000 years ago the moon would have been so close to the earth, it would have fallen onto our planet.

The earth has a magnetic field which is generated by its internal electrical currents (a lot of the earth is composed of iron). This field allows you to use a compass and protects the earth and its inhabitants from harmful solar radiation. The overall strength of this magnetic field was first measured by Karl Gauss in 1835. Since then it has been measured every 10-15 years or so. These measurements have shown that the magnetic field is decaying, just like radioactive elements. The strength of the earth's internal magnet has a half-life of 1400 years, which basically means it halves every 1400 years. This decay is very rapid. It means that, for example, 6000 years ago the magnetic field was a lot stronger than it is now. Going back again, we find that 20,000 years ago the electrical current would have been so strong that the earth could not have withstood the heat produced, and would have been totally liquefied. Therefore the earth is less than 20,000 years old. (The earth is even younger than 20,000 years but this shows how way-out evolution is of course!)

The oceans of the earth also show that they belong to a young earth. For example: many mountains, cliffs and underwater canyons are found below sea level. If the earth was billions of years old, all these would have been flattened out due to erosion. Also recent studies and measurements of coral growth in the oceans reveal coral formations are much younger than initially thought, less than 8,000 years old.

Evolutionists say that the earth-moon system is billions of years old. It has been calculated that if this is the case, there should be miles of dust on the surface of the moon due to meteoric bombardment and the break-up of surface rocks over time. NASA was afraid to send men to the moon, as they would sink deep into the dust. So unmanned probes were sent to analyse the problem. But the dust problem turned out to be totally non-existent. As it is evident from the Apollo landings and the footprints made by astronauts, there is only about 2-3 inches of dust on the surface, indicating an age of around 6-8000 years. Thanks to evolutionary scientists, there is silence on this very strong evidence for a young moon. This again adds to the reality of the Bible.

According to evolutionists, the gas and oil in the earth was trapped there millions and millions of years ago. This gas and oil is trapped in the earth under very high pressures. It is this pressure that causes oil to gush out of oil wells, as soon as it is found. The study of rocks surrounding oil wells indicates that the pressure should have 'bled off' in just a few thousand years. If the evolutionists were right, the pressure in these underground chambers of gas and oil should have dropped to zero long ago, but obviously this is not so. These high pressures show that the earth is young.

The age of past civilizations of the earth should tell us much about how long humans have existed. Evolutionists say that man has been around for about 1 million years, or so. If this were true, the earliest civilizations should reach back quite some time into the past, and we should have many, many written records from hundreds of thousands of years ago. But even the earliest civilizations only go back to 2-3000 BC. These civilizations appeared suddenly and fully developed. This fact again totally fits the Bible. This is a very simple point but very important, yet it can be ignored!

Scientists have searched the earth's rock strata (which was supposed to have been laid down in the last 5 billion years) for craters and meteorite rock, but none have ever been found. This means that the earth would have been avoided by meteors for billions of years or that the earth is young, which is the truth.

The size of the sun has been directly measured at observatories since 1836. According to hundreds of measurements, the sun's diameter is shrinking at a rate of around 0.1% every century, which is equivalent to about 1.5 m per hour. Only 50,000 years ago, the sun would have been so large that our oceans would boil and life could not exist.

Also the sun's own radiation 'pushes' particles less than 100,000th of a centimetre in diameter out of the Solar System. All these microscopic particles should have been blown out of the Solar

System by now, if it really were billions of years old. But satellites find such small particles abundantly in the Solar System, therefore it is young...simple really!

Comets are mainly made up of frozen gases, ice and rocks. So when they are near the sun, the sun evaporates some of these materials, producing a tail. The tail's material is lost in space. So as time goes on normal comets should be gone within several hundred orbits, due to them wearing away. So the short-period comets in our solar system that appear fairly often would have disappeared in less than 10,000 years if evolution were right. There is also no known way to add new comets to the Solar System. Since there are still short-period comets orbiting our sun, the Solar System and comets are young. If these comets were millions of years old, they would have been larger than the sun to start off with! The 'behaviour' and orbits of comets are not consistent with large ages. Comets did not naturally form over billions of years. Comets are young. So is the whole universe.

All the four gas giants: Jupiter, Saturn, Uranus and Neptune have rings. The largest and most familiar are the rings of Saturn. These planetary rings are mainly composed of millions of fragile pieces of solid gases, rocks and water ice. Scientists don't understand how ammonia, which should quickly vaporize into space, could form these delicate rings. They could not have got there from random events and chaos, but were <u>created</u> by a Designer. The rings are also continuously bombarded by meteors and debris from space and it has been calculated that they should have disappeared after about 10,000 years. But they're still there, so planetary rings must be young.

Throughout the universe, hydrogen is being converted into helium. But this is a one-way process: hydrogen cannot be produced in large amounts by the breakdown of other elements. If the universe is as old as evolutionists think, there would be no hydrogen left. So because the universe is mainly composed of hydrogen, it must be young. This fact cannot be denied.

Galaxies cannot rotate as solid bodies, since they are composed of billions of separate stars. The inner stars orbit around the galactic centre faster than the outer ones do. So just one or two revolutions (estimated to be about 100,000-200,000 years) of the galaxy would tighten up the whirlpool-shaped spiral arms, and distort its shape. The galaxies' shape is not yet distorted, therefore the universe is young.

Evolutionists say that because many stars are hundreds of thousands of light years (the distance light travels per year) away from the earth, yet the light from these stars is shining on the earth, then this means the earth must be extremely old. This is simply solved, as I have already shown the Bible is totally accurate and there is nothing it cannot explain, simply because it is the truth. The reason why light from distant stars is shining on the earth is because as the Bible states "God placed lights in the sky to <u>shine on the earth</u>." (Genesis 1: 14-19).

So God made the lights of these massive and distant stars shine on the earth at the time of creation! So that the whole universe could function. So even though light travels at 186,000 miles a second God made the light emitted from distant stars to immediately connect to the earth to be seen by human beings as they are part of creation. Let's not forget that God originally made stars to be beautiful and to set times and dates for events. God did this to give man a 'natural clock'. To this day that is exactly what we do i.e. a year is the earth's cycle of the sun and one month is the moon's cycle of the earth. Dating and time systems were originally based on the sun, moon and stars.

Here is another point I hope you can get your head round: what about pure material like rock for instance? Now rock is obviously extremely important. Without it the world would have no platform to support human life, I mean what would we stand on etc? But my point is: rock in its very nature and structure is old looking. Rock is rock no matter what, so how can a scientist say it is millions or billions of years old? I mean have you ever heard of baby rock? What I am saying is that God made everything perfectly all round the same time so the molecular structure of rock has been purposely made to be strong and give an old aesthetic look, that has been bench-marked by humans to be far, far older than it actually is. Scientists use potassium-argon dating information from rock samples which have been given certain atomic and molecular characteristics by God, in order to do a particular job, which has been interpreted falsely by evolutionistic scientists who have slapped a huge dates on these characteristics to 'fit' the weak evolutionary theory. Let me put it this way: think of cement: when it is not set it is a kind of liquid and its molecular structure different to rock, but when set it instantly becomes different aesthetically and also in its molecular structure. I can guarantee if concrete had never been discovered and you gave a piece to scientists for the first time they would put a massive date on it, just like they have with fossils and other things, yet concrete sets in only hours. This is basically how people are getting confused with potassium-argon dating and evolution thus they are rejecting God's creation. God made things so that they unify together perfectly in a natural way. It seems that whatever science cannot explain it tries to 'hide' in the past. Nature and the whole universe have a 'mature' quality, but man has ultimately forgotten God and used this natural quality as a date for another belief. When God made Adam and Eve they would not have been put on the earth as babies, and the fruit they needed to eat would have come from mature trees. Imagine you are making your garden look good, the first thing you would do is make it look natural, and one of the ways you do this is by making it look old. This is exactly what God did when he made the earth. So when you look at the moon, for example, don't think it is millions of years old, but it has been made to look a particular way to give it its own beauty and natural style. Can you imagine if it was perfectly smooth, what style is that? The moon has actually got tiny bits of spherical glass all over its surface so that it shines at night. Also if these glass bits were perfectly round it would be too bright. It has been designed perfectly to have a balanced natural glow.

So there you have it in a 'nutshell': the earth and the whole universe are young, and evolution and everything that relates to it is a lie. Put simply, it is just a huge hoax.

There is much more information that shows this truth. This is just the tip of the iceberg.

Here are more facts that show how the dinosaurs fit into the truth from the Bible:

We've all heard about dinosaurs, evolving millions of years before man and then being destroyed by a comet but that is total rubbish, and the comet theory is interpreted falsely as explained previously. They did not live millions of years ago and rule the earth because there is much evidence that shows dinosaurs have lived together with humans.....just as the Bible states. Dinosaur comes from the Greek language, which means 'large lizard'. Most of them were huge, some even 15m high, while some of them were as small as birds. They supposedly died out about 65 million years ago. There are various evolutionist theories for their extinction, but none of these theories fit all the facts. In the following, we will see more facts that show dinosaurs did not live long ago at all, as many have been lead to believe.

Fossilized human tracks have been found in Russia and Arizona, and horse tracks in Uzbekistan alongside fossilized dinosaur tracks. **This means that human beings were living at the same as the dinosaurs.** This would not have meant a great threat to people, because most dinosaurs were vegetarians and the carnivorous ones usually preyed on other dinosaurs. Again this fact fits in with the truthful Biblical account of history.

In 1983 a professor of Turkmenia's Institute of Geology reported what appeared to be human footprints. "This spring, an expedition from the Institute of Geology of the Turkmen SSR Academy of Sciences found over 1,500 tracks left by dinosaurs in the mountains in the south-east of the Republic. Impressions resembling in shape to human footprints were discovered next to the tracks of the prehistoric animals."

This example is just one of many other similar findings reported.

At Berea college in Kentucky reports was also made of a human track left in sandstone of the 'Upper Carboniferous Period'. Numerous scientists have investigated these tracks and concluded that they are genuine. In a book tackling this finding an evolutionist writes "If man existed as far back as the Carboniferous Period in any shape, then the whole science of geology is so completely wrong that all the geologists will resign their jobs and take up truck driving. Hence, for the present at least, science rejects the attractive explanation that man made these mysterious prints in the mud of the Carboniferous with his feet."

So really these evolutionists know they are wrong but cannot admit it! Evolutionists have even suggested that these footprints were made by some kind of unidentified amphibian! ....I don't think so.

Another finding of fossilized human tracks alongside dinosaur-tracks reported through the years was found in the Paluxy River area of Glen Rose, Texas. Along with other footprint tracks, these tracks have been the source of considerable controversy. Not far away still in the state of Texas, a set of cogwheel imprints runs alongside a dinosaur track in an area called Dinosaur Flats. Another puzzling feature, for evolutionists, from this same area is the 'hand print in Cretaceous limestone'. This find is currently being studied with a great deal of interest. Even though there are findings such as these, still the main thing that proves the Bible is true is creation itself!

Dinosaur bones have been found un-fossilized which still contain red blood cells and haemoglobin (used to carry oxygen in the blood). These bones were found in Alaska (North shore of Alaska). Not just a handful were found but many thousands. DNA begins to decompose when an animal dies. After about 10,000 years all the DNA in an organism would be gone. Some fragments of DNA were found in supposedly 80 million year-old dinosaur bones. This means that the dinosaur bones are only several thousand years old. What must be remembered here is that fossils look old and are benchmarked as millions of years old by scientists who don't believe in God and global flooding. But the facts are these fossils were formed under ten thousand years ago by the affects of a global flood! It's a bit like the Titanic that sunk in the Atlantic in 1912. When it was finally found in 1973 it was a shock to explorers as it looked 100's of years old yet it had been at the bottom of the Atlantic ocean for only 61 years.

Dinosaur bones are exhibited in textbooks and museums as a proof of evolution. But none of their fossils show evolution happening at all. And their sudden extinction cannot be explained by the theory of evolution. Most dinosaurs died out because of the flood. There is no evidence that they lived 100 million years ago. Dinosaurs are not way back in history as the lie and complete con of evolution would have people believe.

Alligators, crocodiles, monitors (e.g. komodo dragon) all fit the description of dinosaurs as large lizards. There were many types of dinosaurs that were smaller than these reptiles today. Consider the komodo dragon, one of the largest and most fierce land-living reptiles alive today. It is about 3 m long, can outrun a human for short distances, eats deer, hogs, and can be dangerous for a grown man.

In 1977 a Japanese fishing ship caught a large animal carcass in its trawl net near New Zealand. The remains of this creature were hauled on board and examined. This huge monster had been dead for about a month and had started to decompose. It was measured, 5 photos of it were shot by a zoologist (evolutionist), and flipper samples taken. But unfortunately, for fear of contaminating their fresh supply of fish, the Japanese threw this huge monster back into the sea. It was measured to be 10 m long. Its neck was 1.5 m long, its head 45 cm, and the 4 flippers were 1 m in length. The creatures total weight was 4000 pounds (1814 kg).

When the ship got back, and the photos were all developed, they left evolutionary scientists puzzled, because no-one could identify the animal. The flipper samples were analysed and showed that the animal was similar to a fish, or reptile, but not to a mammal. Therefore it could not have been a whale or seal. Its neck was too long to be a fish. Slowly, the idea that it was a plesiosaur (a sea-dwelling dinosaur) grew, since no other animal was found to agree with the data, especially the 4 identical flippers and its large size. Japanese scientists have agreed that it is a plesiosaur.

The New Zealand monster was front-page news for many weeks in Japan. 58 Japanese, South Korean and Russian ships were sent into the area to recover the animal, but it was not found.

Evolutionists try to ignore findings like this. Instead they continue to deceive themselves and others. They call this creature a figment of the imagination - or say it was a shark that somehow decomposed to remarkably resemble a dinosaur! But the 5 photos and flipper samples totally disprove this. <u>Everything</u> points to it being a plesiosaur. There are other reports of dinosaurs living today. These accounts are from scientists and eyewitnesses. For example reports about dinosaurs living in the swamps of Zaire have been known for around three centuries. The ancient legends of dragons is an indication that dinosaurs and men lived together. Almost every culture on earth has some great monster or dragon in its history. The description of these dragons very much resembles that of dinosaurs. Also many stories of knights braving huge dragons can indicate that dragons are not just based on myth.

The Bible mentions two huge animals that were dinosaurs. One is Leviathan which dwelled in the sea (Job 41: 1-34):

'Who can make him open his jaws, ringed with those terrifying teeth? His back is made of rows of shields, fastened together and hard as stone. Light flashes when he sneezes and his eyes glow like the rising sun. Flames blaze from his mouth, and streams of sparks fly out. Smoke pours from his nose, like smoke from weeds burning under a pot. His breath starts fires burning: flames leap out of his mouth. His neck is so powerful that all who meet him are terrified.'

The other is Behemoth who dwelled on land and water. (Job 40:15-19):

'Look at the monster Behemoth; I created him and I created you. He eats grass like a cow, but what strength there is in his body, and what power there is in his muscles! His tail stands up like a cedar and the muscles in his legs are strong. His bones are as strong as bronze and his legs are like iron bars. The most amazing of all my creatures! Only his creator can defeat him. He is not afraid of a gushing river; he is calm when the Jordan dashes in his face. He lies down under thorn bushes and hides among the reeds in the swamp.'

In 1924 some Roman style lead artifacts were excavated near Tucson, and unique carvings were found on these implements, particularly a clear dinosaur depiction on a sword. The Arizona Historical Society still has the sword. Many other artifacts all over the world dating right the way back in history clearly show evidence of the dinosaurs existence at those times by the drawings, carvings and sculptures of them, crafted to fine detail.

Burial stones in Peru were recently discovered by government archaeologists who have found <u>thousands</u> of stones that clearly show men interacting with the dinosaurs, many different species in fact. This is no surprise, because the Bible's account of history is true. You must remember that evolutionists say Man evolved 1 million years ago and dinosaurs 65 million. Anyone can clearly see that evolution is ridiculous.

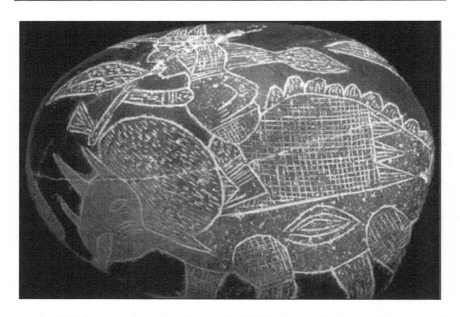

In 1945 an archaeologist called Waldemar Julsrud discovered many clay figurines buried at the foot of El Toro Mountain on the outskirts of Acambaro, Mexico. Eventually over 33,000 ceramic figurines were found in the area and identified with the Chupicuaro Culture who lived around 800 BC to 200 AD. The authenticity of Julsrud's find has been challenged because the huge collection of detailed figures included dinosaurs. So in 1954 the Mexican government sent a team of archaeologists to investigate the find. Julsrud's work has survived numerous tests. Moreover, the dinosaurs are modeled in very agile, active poses, fitting well with the latest scientific evidence and concluding that the artists who modeled them must have actually observed these creatures themselves. Some sauropods are depicted with very distinctive features.

There are many, many other different cases all over the world that clearly show the truth about the Bible, but scientists and other people who teach untruth try to cover them over.

This all proves the Biblical account of history is true.

Chapter 6

Other senseless beliefs and so-called 'mystical forces' EXPLAINED!

Anyway, as you can see, the universe, earth and life was created by God. Mankind sinned and events like the flood were set into motion, and all this truth is pushed aside by most, and the world has become very confused and mixed up. Apart from this many other stupid and senseless beliefs have come into operation: things like superstition, tarot cards, telepathy, star signs, and much more. Basically anything which preaches nonsense that has no truthful structure or rules to live by. So I would like to explain why these senseless beliefs are wrong and the Bible is right.

For starters, the star signs: how can a star which is a lifeless object that can be hundreds or even thousands of light-years away influence someone's personality and life or predict the future? Why do people believe these things and put their hope in them? It's because they have no structure in their minds that is based on truth. People just want instant highs and gossip. Unfortunately they don't realize how weak-minded they are, and to make it worse, some think this is a strength! Star Signs make as much sense as a square wheel on flat ground. There is no logic in such a thing.

People love to 'swallow' such banter because the stars themselves are massive celestial bodies that can be many light years from earth, they are also huge in size, ancient, and can be seen from all over the earth. This must be what mesmerizes people in awe. So saying that their lives on earth relate to these objects gives some 'meaning' to their lives. In other words if something is big and significant, like the stars, people want to relate themselves to them to make them feel important.

We have been created to be social and to have companionship, so if society as a whole talks about such things like star signs people want to talk to other people about it and everyone gets caught up in a massive fantasy illusion that fits their lives because it fits in with everyone else, plus people can't stop their desire to gossip. Half the time anyway people only believe their star sign readings if they are good, and if they are bad they ignore them. Everyone wants to be part of something big but most people only accept if something is big or not on the basis of what others think, not on truth i.e. the Bible is the truth but treated as unimportant to the vast majority of people.

Even after all this false belief many people aren't sure what they believe in. There's nothing solid and 100% in their minds. People seem to go through daydream-like phases in the search for a solid and permanent foundation of happiness, whatever it comes from, as long as it puts a smile on their face. But nothing this world can offer is ever permanent. Many think the only thing that can be 'solid' in life is their houses or finance i.e. material possessions, but of course all that falls to pieces in the end. And as people themselves don't last, what good is money anyway in the long term? No matter how well-made anything is in this world, there will come a time when it will collapse like an old shack and something will be put in its place. The only thing that can last however is a person's understanding of the truth. But many just live their lives day-to-day and don't try to understand what the truth is to all things.

The truth is, beliefs like the star signs are very dangerous. They feed a person's human nature, have no standards, and are easy to live by because anything goes with them. They fit into a corrupt and mixed up society that in turn is full of all kinds of senseless, meaningless teachings and 'philosophies'. It's rather like the flow of a stream: everything is running one way so it's easy to let yourself go in that direction. But the trouble is that the flow is in the direction of an enormous waterfall that will destroy anything which travels that way. The correct way to go is against the current, using a sound guide that is proper, truthful and good. God alone is good. The teaching of the Bible is the way to go, rather like fish that swim upstream, fighting against the current.

These senseless teachings in life cause people to wander near the edge of the path they are supposed to travel as a family together in God's truth. But people like the 'taste' of this world and slip off the path. However, God is the saving ledge that stops you from falling and being drowned in that enormous waterfall of untruth. If people don't listen to the truth that God exists, they become divided and wander around in different directions and claim to know where they are going in life. But the facts are they haven't got a clue and they are too proud and stubborn to admit it.

This world is like a brick wall that is weak or that has great cracks running straight through it. If it is not repaired by someone who cares and wants to do a good job it will fall. Painting it white won't help nor will pretending it is not serious or that it does not need repairing. But using effort to understand the truth with the right mind set will repair the damage.

So senseless teachings are all around us but people don't care because they don't want to look closely into truth as it will hinder their lifestyle. To know the truth and have real knowledge, is to have reverence for God.

Instead people put their 'faith' in lifeless objects i.e. money, the stars, tarot cards, charms and idols etc....etc and many other types of things that are of no substance at all. Some children have more sense. The trouble is many adults can think that anything which makes <u>money</u> is grown up and mature. People allow themselves to be subject to many untruthful ways of thinking and go with the flow, because they think there is no dynamic consequence for thinking so stupidly, and then they say it's just a bit of fun. Isn't that what children say when playing chicken on the roads or a train track?

People can think it's tough to do what they should not and weak to do what they should. Typical human nature. Because doing what you should do means to abide by laws and rules, but people don't do that because they want to be a law unto themselves and break laws and rules to put themselves above the law. It's all to do with pride and hate. Someone who's very proud of themselves won't listen to rules because they want to make rules of their own and rebel. This is one of many ways of how people treat the Bible. Not only do people treat the Bible this way but also worldly laws that have been put into motion by the government to try and help people i.e. the police. Many laws of the world have come through the ages and are derived from the Bible, but have slowly been bent and corrupted so there are now many worldly laws in operation that are wrong. All this just increases Mans' confusion and mess.

Because the governments of this world have slowly drifted away from the foundation of good, and allowed themselves to abide by other standards, regulations and rules of power, they have ultimately neglected the truth from which all good and righteous laws originated from. They have no understanding of truth and cannot filter out the false teachings and untruth or lies that rise up in society. Therefore God's laws and ways are pushed out and Mans' ways are added instead. People forget God and think they can do what they want because Mans' laws don't say they are wrong. So not only do senseless teachings affect the way people think about God and truth, but they are backed up by the fact that nothing is said about them in political and social debates. This is why things like star signs and the like are allowed ground, because the only laws against them comes from knowing the truth, but the truth is not given the power it should have as it is being separated from the laws of government.

Another big part in the belief of senseless teachings is that like evolution, peoples' imaginations make them seem plausible. For instance the human mind is capable of imagining that impossible things are possible. But just because the human mind can imagine many things it does not mean they can happen. The trouble is the imagination can be dangerous if it is not guided by common sense and the right mind set. As we all know, people who take powerful drugs can hallucinate and their imaginations can go wild. Some can think they are capable of impossible feats and so harm themselves and others. It's the same with alcohol people can become warped and stupid. It's also the same even without drugs: for instance if a talented sports player becomes too proud of themselves, they can start to become over-confident and thus imagine they are capable of things they can't do. Also the way in which a person is educated can affect the imagination and they can thus become deluded if they are told things that are not true. People can become 'drunk' with imagination in many different ways. It's much to do with the way people are educated and how they treat and use their imaginations.

This drunk imaginative state is the way many are living, but the trouble is they enjoy being like this because it feels good and suits their lives. These people aren't basing their understanding on truth but on the foundation that it is easy to think with the majority who conform to human nature and ignore Godly understanding. Becoming drunk to God's creation and ignoring it is very foolish.

Here are some examples that show this drunk imaginative state of mind: People can think that seeing a certain number of magpies will affect their lives or tell them the future. What?...I'm sorry, but they are just birds! How can a bird do anything else apart from being a bird?.......There are also a lot of other people who don't believe such banter, yet if you think about it, they believe that a magpie created itself if they believe in evolution or are an atheist.

Some people believe that cards or crystal balls put out on a table by a person with a husky, mystical voice who pretends to have some kind of ability to know the future via the cards or ball, is the basis of truth. But this has no truthful structure and makes no sense. How can cards do this? They are just cards! How can a crystal ball do this? It's just a ball of crystal! It's a lame lie that is used on weak-minded people to gain money. This lie drives people away from the truth about God and Christ. God is a real being as I have explained and he exists in the spiritual realm which is unseen. God himself can do all things, but bits of paper or a shiny ball can't....simple. Anything that is not to do with God and Christ Jesus is a lie.

What makes this worse is that the people who perform this kind of junk can start to think that the inanimate objects they use are actually revealing something. Ultimately they fool themselves! Obviously cards are just bits of paper. Paper is made from trees that are sawn down then taken to a factory that then makes them into cards. A crystal ball is a piece of crystal made into a ball shape.

This same kind of drunkenness is in the senseless belief of reading tea-leaves. This must have originated from someone with an overactive imagination who had nothing else better to do than look at the tea leaves at the bottom of their cup. I really do feel very sorry for folk who think tea-leaves can tell them things. It's a good thing that most people make tea from tea bags nowadays.

Some people believe breaking a mirror will give seven years bad luck! A mirror is a piece of glass with a metallic silver backing that reflects light. When it breaks you hear a smashing sound which in turn lets you know it has broken. It is not alive, it cannot see, hear, walk or talk. It's a material object that has no life.

Some people think that black cats crossing their path will give good or bad luck. But they should know that when a cat crosses their path it means that a cat has just walked by. Anyway why just cats? Why not crisp bags or other bits? If you believe things like these please re-examine the way you think. If you know someone who does, please give them this book. Teachings like these give a persons mind the strength of poorly-set jelly.

Fortune tellers are people who don't understand what they are doing, but are just acting on the desire for money and the image of mystery and the so-called unexplainable to get fame, and become proud of themselves. But the simple facts are they are tricksters and generally say what people want to hear. They in turn don't believe in God or Christ. They push people away from God by confusing their minds. They confuse people because they are stating in their actions that supernatural abilities have nothing to do with God. So people think anything supernatural is a mystery, thus God and Christ are canceled out. Yet it is God's power that enables truthful miracles and truthful supernatural things to happen (some people who don't believe in God and Christ can perform supernatural acts but they are not truthful. I will shortly go on to explain the reason for this).

When Christ was on earth, he performed incredible miracles

that had never been seen before to show that he was the son of God. He did not say he was doing it himself. How can we do supernatural things by our minds alone? But rather he said he was doing it by the power of God. We must remember here that this power is clearly seen in creation. Creation shows God and Christ showed the truth about God. That is why I wrote earlier that anything that is not truthful and not linked to God and Christ is a lie that ultimately pushes you away from belief in them.

So let's examine the facts again: senseless teachings need more thought and should be shown for what they really are namely lies and destructive tricks. Thinking that miracles can be done by the 'power of the mind' alone is senseless, of course. But there is another fact that needs to be brought into play here that makes this all a lot clearer. Can you think what it is?

It is simple really but you need to be Biblically-minded to think it. This is what is missing: as I wrote previously mankind sinned at the time of creation, but was fooled by an angelic being that lead mankind into disobeying God. Well, this angelic being is <u>still</u> fooling people today. At the time of creation God made many angels and some of them rebelled against God, with one main angel as ruler. His name at that time was Lucifer but now he is called Satan. What must be remembered here is that Satan and his fallen angels have the power to perform untruthful miracles. God gave them these powers not to be abused but to fit in with his plan for humanity, but because they rebelled and have thus been condemned, they are using there abilities to try to cancel out God from the human race, and thus separate man from God. What they are trying to do is confuse man by engineering all these false teachings and lies via Mans' stupidity and human nature.

Many years ago magicians and tricksters would perform false miracles and then convince people that this was the work of the 'real' god. Then people would start to believe them and in turn worship that 'god'. This would push them away from the true God of the Bible. This has been happening in much the same way ever since the fall of mankind through sin. Although times have changed, human nature hasn't and people are still easily lead and fooled, simply because they do not examine and keep in mind the truth about God.

Remember people can say that they perform miracles by the 'power of the mind', but they can't explain creation and how they were made, so no matter how you look at it God is always in the picture because he made all things. So saying that God does not exist is untrue. Thinking that supernatural things can happen by 'the power of the mind' alone implies that Christ performed his miracles in the same way. This warped way of thinking can cause people to doubt Christ and the Bible, and stops them from learning the truth. This is exactly what Satan is trying to achieve for humanity. Things like these cause the truth of the Bible to be doubted and are part of an unseen angelic world of cunning trickery.

There are many things in the world that defy nature: some people read minds, perform impossible tricks and can bend objects without touching them. Some practice black magic and things like voodoo and cause 'unexplained' phenomena. Most are bewildered by such events and either laugh them off, or just like to be entertained by them. Some are so confused that they don't even try to understand why.

These things are all the work of supernatural spirits that are fallen angels, who's goal is to try to stop people believing in Christ Jesus and God. That is why these things happen to confuse people and get people to believe that Biblical events are not to do with God. That the world is full of 'unexplained' things. That's exactly how Satan wants mankind to think; in fact any belief as long as it is not the truth. So with this in mind we can examine a much clearer picture.

As explained these fallen angels want people to believe that impossible things are capable of happening by thinking about them to confuse people about God's true miracles and the Bible. Telepathy and psychic power etc, are lies. Think about it: when someone wants to do something, what good will just thinking about it do? Will this make it happen? Of course not! There is no difference in thinking of doing something, than that of someone who is to supposed to have 'psychic power' by thinking of doing something – the two are the same. We are all human beings; thinking itself is immensely complex and has all been designed by the creator. This is plainly obvious. Human beings cannot move objects with their minds. <u>There are no hidden powers of the mind</u> - psychic powers are non-existent. There are however supernatural beings i.e. angels, (which rebelled against God) that can make it look that way, to trick people into being confused about so-called mind power, because that in turn gives the impression that Christ used his 'mind power' and was a psychic. It's a simple trick that tries to make Christ and the miracles of the Bible fade into the background. **If you are confused and mislead by one supernatural miracle you are confused about them all.** When Christ was on earth he did not say that he performed miracles by the power of his mind....no! Rather he said it was by the power of God working through him (John 14: 11-13). As I have explained earlier God can do all things, apart from wrongdoing. So there is a deadly deception in the world which aims to simply push out Christ Jesus from peoples' lives by means of many lies and confusion. The trouble is many people are so confused that they don't even realize they are.

So much of society has been mislead to believe that mind power and hidden powers of the mind are real. They believe that if a person focuses their mind strongly on something it can happen. But think of the last time you were hungry. Did a meal make itself in front of your eyes, because you thought about it a lot? Think of all the starving people in the third world. Their one thought can be food. Now think of someone who could give aid saying to these people "We will not help you because by the power of your minds you can feed yourselves, just focus."

I think you will have to agree that saying this is insane and if a person believes this they need help. This is the kind of person that would buy a bike with square wheels. Thinking that something will happen of its own accord is no different to this. It shows weak mind-edness and stupidity. Even if you believed it would happen, what difference would that make? The only time thought makes a differ-ence is when you think that something will happen by believing in God's power, because that is real, and the truth that can be trusted.

Even if people could move and control things with their minds, you still could not rule out God's existence, as he would have had to create them in the first place. So why do people think that God is non-existent and physic power real? Basically, there is no excuse not to believe.

So any miracle or wonder that does not give glory to God and Jesus Christ is a lie. In other words when someone is healed without the mention or connection to Christ Jesus and the true God it is a false healing. This falseness can lead the so-called healer to believe they are somehow capable of doing these things by themselves or by false gods or some kind of mystical force. But unknowingly to them they are all complete nonsense! All this deception is really the work of lying spirits who are trying to cancel out God's power and truth.

One of the problems is that people are too easily wowed and amazed by miracles and wonders. Rather they should be more concerned as to whether or not the principles involved in miracles and wonders make sense. However the lying spirits (fallen angels) of this world counterfeit miracles and wonders in all types of different beliefs to get people thinking that their belief is 'true'. It's like algebra in maths: once you know the formula it's easy to work out the answer (truth), or gets easier in time.

Think how incredibly complex the human body is. Now think about someone in a wheelchair who cannot walk, and the reason they can't walk is because it would be too difficult for them to be made well by men. Many operations can never take place as they would be impossible for men. So why is it then that some people are healed without medical aid?.......Simple. It is obviously not the ability of surgeons but of God. Many people get healed by God, and this can increase their faith in him; it is simply the same power that made all things. Unfortunately some people dismiss God's true miracles as 'power of the mind'. If this were so how can someone perform things like this, via their mind, if they are not aware of how to do it? Would surgeons operate if they did not have the skill and understanding that takes many years to master? Also how can so-called positive thinking, which is also just thought, do this?

If God did not have the knowledge of how to heal someone, how could he use his power to do this? Simple, he would not be able to, but God knows all things and is able to do miracles. So miracles show a divine intelligence behind them. Things that are impossible for man are not impossible for God.

It is also believed by some that the earth and certain elements from it have strange forces in and around them which can control a persons' destiny and cause mysterious events etc. But if this were true, how would they work? They simply cannot work, as intelligence is needed to control complex circumstances and heal etc. Forces that are real like magnetism and gravity etc will simply remain as they are. This is all they will be and can be. Teachings about fictional forces like positive and negative energy and many more have no truth in them. Proper, reasonable and realistic explanations cannot be found. Part of the reason for this delusion and perception people are in is because of too many false explanations of supernatural events that are shown through television, cinema and the whole world media.

Real natural forces of the earth have been intelligently made by God to serve a purpose. Magnetism has other uses other than man-made mechanical devices. Migrating birds use star patterns or magnetism to guide them in flight for navigation. The birds use the magnetism to guide them like a compass. Other animals have been created to have certain abilities that use the electromagnetic spectrum to feed and survive. God's immense understanding has designed such creatures. So magnetism and the like are part of creation just like gravity and inertia. We need them. Natural forces are obviously not intelligent and they never could be! But stupid and unthinking people take the true facts about forces and warp them by inventing new ones which go beyond the boundaries of reality i.e. psychic power, magic, astrology, new age paganism, acupuncture, healing bands, crystals, superstitions, negative and positive energy and much, much more imaginary junk.

This shows that people want to live their lives according to what **they** want and believe any old junk as long as it lets them do this. This weak-mindedness is then passed down to the younger generation etc and it becomes second nature for people to have this mind-set.

It is very important to care that we understand this life in truth.

The Bible is the truth, it does not just explain a few points in life it explains **everything** of vital importance. Also, as shown, you now know that God is the truth. Nothing else fits the bill and makes sense. God has purposely made it so that the whole of creation shows his existence and divine intelligence.

So intelligence has to be behind miracle healings, and many other supernatural phenomena. However some is the work of God and some is the work of Satan and the other fallen angels. God is trying to reveal the truth and Satan is trying to cover it up.

So the whole world is bound up in chains of lies, confusion, distraction and disbelief in the truth. But the Bible explains it all and not one thing is left in the dark. Everything we need to know becomes plain and easy to see. So here is a list of some so-called unexplained phenomena, with a truthful explanation of what they are and why they are happening.

Ghosts

Many people think that there is such a thing as ghosts; some don't care, but almost all people would feel uneasy if they were left alone in a big house in the middle of nowhere. Part of that fear comes from not understanding what these things are. The answer is simple: ghosts are really deceptive spirits (fallen angels) that are trying to convince people that spirits of the dead have no connection to the Bible but wander in a limbo-like state around the world. This in turn gives no emphasis to God and heaven, but again confuses people to think that they will live after they die and may find peace without the belief of Jesus Christ. In the Bible it explains in full detail why people are not left on the earth in this way. It has perfect reasons but the trouble is people do not read it. Many people have seen supernatural things like this but don't want to discuss it, as they are afraid of what others think or are so confused they ignore it.

Some people think that when a relative or friend dies they watch over them but this is simply not true. I feel sorry for people who think like this because they are trying to find some kind of comfort in a person's death but unfortunately the comfort they give themselves is a lie. It is faith in Jesus Christ that enables a person to live after death in perfect happiness and that alone. That is why deceptions like these are so bad as they cancel out the most important thing of all - <u>Christ</u>. Also people who contact the dead are not doing what they think they are as they are not contacting the spirits of dead people but rather fallen angels. A lot of the time these spirits mimic the personality of the deceased person and make out that they are fine and well. This is a massive trick because the person who hears this will be in an emotional state and more than likely be convinced they are hearing from this dead person. Also they will be consumed by memories and powerful feelings, and will be glad to hear a positive message. But the truth is very different because people who are involved in 'contacting the dead' like this have no solid grasp of the truth (The Bible – God's word - and the only sound guide) and the people they try to 'contact' are people who have never known God, so when these spirits say that everything is OK they are lying to deceive people into thinking peace and life are all part of dying even if you do not know Christ. If you don't think Jesus Christ is important you won't look for him.....this is a simple but very deadly trick.

Ghosts are pushed into society at a very young age. Children's programmes can be full of spooky characters and stories which starts the confusion process very early. Some ghost stories are more graphic and can have long lasting-effects on how people perceive supernatural activities which don't relate to God. Also many children can start to develop unhealthy fears. They can start to put pieces together to 'explain' why things like this occur using false ideas and lies which have a powerful and lasting effect from a young age.

There is much supernatural activity that happens all over the world every day that clearly shows the presence of the angels, whether good or bad, in society. But even then people write these events off and pursue their own interests, and don't think these things through properly. I won't even list all the things that show supernatural activity - the list is enormous. But here are some pictures taken in Egypt of figures appearing, seen by millions.

Wizards, witchcraft, and magicians

There are many who find wizardry and witchcraft interesting, because it can be broadcast in the whole public media to look good. There are programmes on television and also films that show wizardry and witchcraft as harmless fun. People of all ages swallow it up failing to realize it is based on a massive deception to cancel out God and Christ. There are also many magicians who use these kinds of ways to make money by baffling people in wonder and amazement. Some magicians are not as bad as others and use basic practical tricks to entertain. But ultimately almost all these forms of wonder and entertainment can lead and grow into terrible confusion and serve as obstacles to stop people from understanding the truth that comes from God. The truth is many of these things are 'helped along' by a higher force of beings which use peoples' ignorance to engineer the world's mind-set to be deceived and confused. These beings are the fallen angels as previously explained. They can use people in different ways, some to make films and television programmes which serve untruth, while others are used to perform baffling acts and feats, to throw the truth about Christ out of the picture. This all again relates to the above: people believe in some 'mystical force' that allows people to do supernatural things, but this is really Satan and his angels working unseen. So Satan keeps himself hidden so as not to reveal himself, otherwise he would reveal the truth about God and who he really is. So he stays cloaked in 'darkness'. He moves around unseen in a world of lies and cunning deception.

As a result of lies many folk think that Christ was a magician or some kind of wizard, or warlock.

If miracles and wonders are performed without the mention or association to the truth i.e. God and Christ people will automatically think that God and Christ are non-existent or are misconceptions of another 'truth'.

Again it must be underlined here that the angels are not human beings but angelic beings who have been given superhuman abilities, which enable them to perform miracles and other feats. This power was created by God who made them. The angels were made to co-exist with mankind in the unseen spiritual realm, and live in peace with us (as explained). But some of them rebelled and started to abuse their authority and have thus been condemned, but as the Bible states God will deal with them fully at a time he has set. So these spirits try to make out that men can perform tricks and other feats by themselves to hide the truth and ultimately 'explain' that the unexplained is nothing to do with God. They do not want human beings to know God by believing in Jesus Christ and thus be redeemed from sin and the power of death. So witchcraft, magicians and wizards are all lies to confuse and muddle up peoples' thoughts when it comes to the truth.

Aliens and U. F. O's

Let's start with a clear statement: aliens are **not real.** They are fallen angels that manifest themselves this way to again confuse the thoughts of man and push out God's truth. For example some people actually think Christ was an alien!

The Bible says that God made the universe, man and woman and all life on <u>earth,</u> so making out that other forms of life exist elsewhere makes the Bible look untrue and uncompleted. It can also start other insane arguments and cause divisions. Even some people who believe in the Bible think that God created other races of physical beings, which live on other planets in space, which is totally untrue. God only created the human race the Bible explains and there are many, many important and dynamic reasons why he made just human beings in his image and also why it is impossible for other beings like this to exist. For example here's just one: when Adam sinned the <u>whole universe and everything in it</u> was subjected to death so how could this tie in with other beings? They would have been condemned for no reason, and this is impossible as God is truthful and not unfair. So believing there are other beings in the universe is total garbage. The reason why all human beings die is because we are born from mortal parents who in turn 'inherited' sin which has ran through generations all the way back to Adam and Eve who were cursed with death in their bodies for their sin.

'Aliens' are also there as a future tool that Satan will use to falsely explain away future Biblical events that are going to take place. These events will be so powerful that the world will change to a new order almost 'overnight'. One of these events is called 'The Rapture' in which God will take all the people who belong to him (those who believe in Jesus Christ, who died and rose again for the sins of the world) who are scattered all over the earth. These people will literally vanish from the face of the earth and no one will be able to find them because God will have taken them away to Christ.

Much of the world has organizations and technology that is used to track or find out about U.F.O's. The truth is that the superpower nations <u>do not know</u> what they are dealing with, hence the secrecy. Under this assumed cloak of secrecy they don't appear foolish to the people and to their enemies, and are thus able to manoeuvre politically.

The phenomenon of genuine 'corn circles' is also an intriguing one, as they relate to 'U.F.O' sightings. Some 'crop circles' are made by humans to 'mimic' the 'real ones' which, under examination, are not even walked on and each stalk shows no bruising.

These large scale feats of plant manipulation and patterning are impossible for human beings, but not of course for the fallen angels. So the crop circles made by people are counterfeits of the ones made by fallen angels, which in turn are hoaxes to fool people.

Crop circles are made overnight and appear the next day leaving most people absolutely baffled. But the truth is that many of the circles and U.F.O's are near pagan tumuli and on ley lines connected with ancient pagan astrological constructions like stone circles. Clearly the spirits (fallen angels) involved are trying to draw investigators and the public into occultic pagan systems of belief, and to be intrigued by false mystical explanations.

The Bible talks about angels occupying certain regions and territories and this again ties in with earth's history. For example in areas where there is usually a lot of false belief or a history of it there can be many 'U.F.O' sightings because there are fallen angels that occupy these regions. Sometimes however you will get random 'U.F.O' sightings but on average you see this basic pattern of appearances.

Remember that U.F.O's and extra terrestrial life make <u>no sense at all</u> and hold no truth whatsoever. They do not explain anything but rather cast 'shadows' on everything.

Here is a list of some reasons why they are total lies and why people can 'hold on' to these deceptions:

1. Nothing else explains the full truth except the Bible, anything else that has 'loose ends' is no more than a lie.

2. The Bible dynamically explains the structure of human existence on earth from two people who God created to the present day. No stone is left unturned.

3. As explained, everything has been created by God and <u>only</u> the human race was created in his image, so how can aliens exist as they were not created in the first place?

4. If you believe there is no creator and God of all things, how were all things made? Even if aliens did exist, **how can a physical being create itself ?** Anything that is physical has to have some

point in its past where it was not alive but put together and made i.e. like human beings in their mother's womb.

5. Alien concepts explain nothing about why we have life, death, good, bad, right, wrong, love, hate, and the beauty and meanings in nature. They also give no meanings as to why human nature is the way it. But the Bible of course does because it is true. The Bible explains everything about the human heart and the right way to live. It teaches goodness and tells you about God. It shows love for mankind and many know that the way the Bible teaches you to live is right and pure. It explains about sin and wrong-doing and there is so much structure and truth in it that you realize immediately (rather you should) that it is superhumanly written and explains all things. Alien concepts explain nothing like this.

6. Remember there can be many lies but only <u>one truth</u>, and the Bible is the one truth.

7. 'Alien abductions' are always weird and 'twisted', which shows the wicked nature of the fallen angels, because they have no goodness in them and naturally act out sin and evil. That's why people who experience so-called 'alien abductions' have very unpleasant and frightening experiences, often horrific. Many of the abductees are painfully and disgracefully 'operated' on and sexually abused while apparently on board U.F.O's. Some also experience flash-backs of the abduction and suffer great depression.

8. Brad Steiger, an American non-Christian who is an investigative journalist, has a book called 'Flying Saucers Are Hostile', and he concludes that 'aliens' have no love for humanity and are in fact hostile to it.

9. There have been some 'U.F.O' sightings in broad daylight over the world in very public areas, some of which have ended in some believers in Jesus Christ and God catching a glimpse, and some of these people have shouted out in the name of Jesus Christ for the 'U.F.O' to go and it has actually vanished in sight of every-

one. Again this shows the truth behind these so-called phenomena.

10. U.F.O's also have also been seen over fields of cattle and other kinds of livestock, but shortly after this takes place the animals are found dead with organs and bits missing. This deception tries to imply that the U.F.O's involved are experimenting just like human abductees cases tell. Again this shows the vile and sinister nature of the fallen angels, because when they deceive it is always done through evil and can never be done through any good.

11. Some people who have seen a 'U.F.O' can be so mesmerized, shocked and stunned that they think they have seen part of a bigger truthful picture. Many almost feel enlightened, and consider themselves important in witnessing an event of such importance to the 'mystery' of the universe and humanity. Thus they become biased and proud and would not like the idea that they have been fooled. A lot of people who frequently study U.F.O's usually have witnessed some kind of event or the aftermath of events. So U.F.O's fuel peoples pride and bias, causing them to be against God's teachings. They can be desperate to explain the Bible away as it hinders what they want to believe.

12. Some abductees claim that 'aliens' have spoken to them, and said they are from 'other dimensions'. But the truth is there is no such thing as other physical dimensions - there is only the spiritual and the physical realms which God made. These 'aliens' (fallen angels) say this to counterfeit truthful spiritual explanations and events. To push away the truth about themselves and who they really are and where they really came from thus covering the truth about Jesus Christ, God and salvation. This deception rules out God, exchanges the truth about God for lies and can explain the Bible in falseness, thus ruling out the spiritual realm and replacing it with another 'physical dimension'.

13. If you don't know the truth about U.F.O's your mind becomes full of mystery and this way of thinking can keep people very interested. It's like a murder mystery story: people love them

because it occupies the mind and keeps you guessing and interested. But as soon as it is all revealed what do people want to do? Watch another one of course. That's how it is with U.F.O's. People in a way want the mystery and interest over and over again rather than one solid explanation. This way of thinking can affect some in why they study and believe in U.F.O's.

So now you know the truth. There is more to go through but for now as long as you see that it is all a 'square wheel' that will do.

U.F.O's are not alien flying saucers but flying squares. (wheels that is).

U.F.O = Untruthful, fake objects.

Angels and demons

In much of the world's history there is much reference to angels and demons. Throughout history angels are the subjects of many works of art, books and many other forms of literature and documentation. So too are demons. This is all linked of course to the truth about the world, from the Bible.

The trouble is much of society 'writes off' angles and demons as old stories and legends, but this is simply not true. Many who believe in the Bible nowadays are weak in what the Bible teaches and don't bring up all the facts about angels and demons that need to be explained in society. They are ultimately afraid of what others will think of them.

God himself has many angels who carry out his good will for humanity. God's own angels do not try to deceive anyone. They battle and fight against Satan and his angels (demons) who are trying to deceive everyone on earth. Many of these spiritual beings work through and with the principles that govern human existence and the universe.

Some angels can influence peoples' feelings and can engineer the way people think and behave through the principles they serve whether good or bad. So fallen angels can dynamically structure circumstances and events to make men become as sinful, wrong and as blind as possible. God's angels on the other hand can assist man to obey God according to his will.

Some angels have the power to put thoughts into the minds of men, and there are different types that have different abilities. Satan and his angels abuse their power and use it to deceive men, but God governs all things and is ultimately in control. God's angels carry out his will and obey his truthful, loving nature. There is a lot more dynamic structure to the way all this works but at this stage it would be too much to take in. As long as you remember that God is in control, ruling with Christ Jesus, that's what really counts.

Satan's angels can give prosperity to people and fame etc. Usually they give this to people who have no idea about the truth of this world in order that other people envy them and want to copy them, and have what they have. But this is all a trick to demonstrate a false happiness, to make people think that happiness is not from God and that you don't need him in your life or Christ Jesus. In other words if you are 'happy' and do not know Christ you're really displaying to others that you don't need Christ and nor do they. But people really need Christ more than they know, and belief in that is true happiness.

The spirits (fallen angels) can also engineer the way in which people interact sexually and can cause much sin and trouble working through peoples' weakness and lack of knowledge and faith in God.

We have all heard about people with evil spirits in them and possession. This again is the fallen angels causing trouble, death and confusion. Also one of the tricks these spirits do is to make out that people who believe in Christ Jesus, God and the Bible are mad. For instance, a lot of people who are possessed can wear ragged clothes and have long hair and be very dirty, smelly etc. They walk around towns and cities alone ranting and raving or muttering rapidly all the time and some quote a lot of Biblical scripture and mention Biblical things or hold crosses. This is a simple trick to make the truth about God look like madness and also the people who proclaim God's message as crazy. This has a very powerful affect on people and can ruin peoples' perception of God and the Bible, even so far as to make it look totally evil, which could not be further from the truth.

There are many cults, organizations and groups that have been influenced by evil demonic power which serve and have served to give God a bad name and make his word look untrue. Many cults and groups have come and gone, some even calling themselves 'churches' which can have bizarre initiation ceremonies and strange evil beliefs. All of which are really controlled by demonic forces (fallen angels) who copy certain elements of the Bible, particularly animal sacrifices, burned offerings and the shedding of blood also many other Biblical things, in order that these evil groups are related to God's truth, thus making God's word look evil and strange. Animal sacrifices, burned offerings and the like are from the Old Testament which was before the time of Christ. After Christ came into the world the law changed and people did not have to live by all the old laws and regulations in the Old Testament because God dealt with sin once and for all through Christ's own sacrifice. So because of the relation to Biblical things people can think the Bible is strange and evil too. For example many false and evil cults have used crosses as a sign of their fellowship. This has a direct and powerful link to Christ as the cross is a strong Biblical image. Other cults also use the Star of David as an evil pentagram which has power to unleash terrible evil. These kinds of ideas have also been used in films, books, and television etc, all over the word.

The angels have great power and many different abilities which they have used through generations to help or hinder the entire world from the time of creation to this very day. Imagine if you had the power of invisibility. That alone would give you tremendous hidden power, but not only do the angels have this but they also have the power to perform miracles and wonders. They can also influence and manipulate the mind <u>without</u> a person being aware. Another extremely complex and unique ability that some angels have is the power to manifest themselves in different forms. Angels that are deceptive however use forms such as U.F.O's, extra terrestrial beings, ghosts and much more. Also if that weren't enough, they don't die like human beings or become tired, hungry, thirsty, sleepy or weary, they can move through the air i.e. fly, and they know the truth about God. This all these supernatural abilities show the incredible creative power of God, with which he made all things both spiritual and physical. But this power is being misused and abused by the fallen angelic beings. God's angels however are on the side of truth and work for the causes of righteousness.

The spiritual realm is not unorganized: there are rules and principles that govern the interaction of these beings with humanity, and God is ultimately in control.

This is basically how angels and demons work, and this shows why there are many phenomena over the world that cannot be explained and why there is so many different evil beliefs and confusion about truth.

Hypnosis

Hypnosis is a subject that many people are confused about, yet a lot don't realize they are. But the truth is simple:

Hypnosis can in many cases put a person completely under the hypnotist's power (or so is thought). We must understand here that for a person's mind to be taken over and controlled, (often becoming a different personality or behaving like an animal) is the works of extreme intelligence. For starters it takes a person's own intellect to control their body, so the same applies to hypnosis. In other words it is the works of another consciousness, or being(s) that are able to interact with the human mind. The beings that are doing this are fallen angels that are trying to confuse the thoughts of mankind.

There are many hypnotists who have appeared on television and all over the media. Virtually all people who are hypnotized have no memory of what happened or if they do it is fuzzy and vague, yet they have had no drugs of any kind. Also many who later see themselves on video cannot believe it is them. But what they don't realize is that they were under the control of deceptive angels who have God-given abilities to interact with the mind. The human mind is extremely complex and far, far, far more complex than anything on earth. People all over the world have studied the brain, yet they still can't even grasp simple concepts of how it functions so well. This again all shows God's incredible intellect and power.

So when people are subject to hypnosis there is no way the quiet voice of a hypnotist could instantly control their whole mind!

That's rubbish! Put it this way, if the television volume was on very low, rather like a hypnotist's voice, and you just made out someone talking about wild bore, would you:

A. Start acting like a wild pig?
B. Turn the volume up?

Somehow I think you would turn the volume up. Do you see what I mean? People are being fooled by the most ridiculous lies! Some people fall asleep at the click of a hypnotist's fingers or change personality. This is of course totally unnatural and impossible! Can't people see this? But what makes this deception even worse is the entertainment and comical value that is linked to the lie. It is human nature to laugh at such things but not understand them, because if people did understand they would not be laughing. So people can laugh at hypnotism, but it is really a deadly trick to stop God from being known. The fallen angels do this because they know that if they make people unsure and confused about 'mystical powers and forces' people will add the Bible to that. So the truth is drowned out by the fact it is linked to the confusion of the world. So in turn people live in an 'unexplained' state. Also because multitudes of people live this way, many think there is no harm in thinking like this. As long as they feel good and satisfy what they want, they are 'happy'.

Remember to control and manipulate the mind is extremely complex. It takes intelligence and power, rather like computer hackers who use their abilities in a wrongful way to tap into complex and sophisticated computer systems to gain access and control. In the same kind of way the multitudes of angels God made can (as previously written) interact and govern the events of mankind through powerful principles. In other words he made angels to, as it were, steer the course of mankind. A massive part in this is the power to interact unseen through the human mind, so God gave some angels this ability. So the truthful answer in a 'nut shell' is: Hypnosis is an evil deception that entertains people to a high degree.

Before we move on to the next chapter I would like to mention the following:

The best thing to do after you have read this book is read the Bible for yourself (If you have not already got Biblical understanding or want to strengthen it) and use this book as a reference to guide the way you think, because society is not focusing on the truth and people are building on the foundations of nonsense.

The truth about God can only be seen by those who 'see' with their minds, not just their eyes. So as I said before, God's creative works are all around us but ultimately people are misinterpreting this which is Satan's will for humanity. God however wants all to believe in him by believing in Jesus Christ, the son of God who came down to earth in human form, to die for the sins of mankind, and anyone who believes this will live spiritually forever.

This, like I said, is no fairy tale but very serious truth. The truth about God is plain. It's like looking at a shiney coin at the bottom of shallow water. The coin is reflecting the light of God's truth but the Devil comes along and dips his hand into the water very slowly then all of a sudden starts to thrash his hand into the mud at the bottom, which clouds the water and stops people from seeing clearly. Over time the mud starts to settle so he does this over and over again all the time working through generations of people, clouding their thoughts with deception and lies. The thing to do is this: see the coin now. It is in what I am writing and in the evidence of creation and truth. Don't leave the coin in the water. Bend down and stretch out your arm, then with your hand take it out! In other words believe in God, examine the truth and take it into your heart and start a relationship with God by believing in Christ Jesus.

(If you already believe I hope this book has so far strengthened your faith and made your mind clearer).

Chapter 7

Tracks of truth, left by the round wheel.

The history of the Bible is very important because it shows how God dealt with us and helped us in the past, leading up to the present day. As I said before, there are many lies but only one truth. Now imagine the truth as a long bicycle wheel track through earth, and lies represented as other tracks. The way you tell which is true or not is by the marks left. For example, every false teaching and lie that is made is like a bike with square wheels that leaves ridiculous marks and haywire lines that do not soundly fit together. But the truth is a single unbroken 'track' that makes sense and goes as far back as we can see. In other words the history of truth has <u>no</u> imperfection to it at all. So here is some more information about the history of the human race that shows that the truth about God from the Bible goes far back into history at all points of time. There are <u>no</u> <u>unexplained points</u> in history but rather God does not stop guiding mankind. Thus there are no breaks in the track.

So here is another totally explained so-called 'mystery'. Around the world many bones and full skeletons of **giant humans** have been found, yes, giant humans! This is no mystery and easy to explain. In the Bible just after mankind's fall (sin) human beings began to spread over the earth (as mentioned). Then the Bible states that some of the fallen angels (who have particular supernatural abilities) chose some women of that time, and changed certain D.N.A characteristics so that the children they bore would grow to become giants, thus creating a giant race of human beings (Genesis 6: 1-4). So in time many generations of people who were giants came from the women which the angelic beings interacted with. (Genesis 6: 4) "In those days, and even later, there were giants on the earth who were descendants of human women an the heavenly beings."

There are also accounts in the Bible of giant humans who lived after the time of the flood. One of which being the famous battle between David and Goliath. In case you do not know, David became one of the kings of Israel and Goliath was a Philistine giant who stood 9 feet tall and had six fingers on each hand. Unfortunately the battle of David and Goliath can be treated as a made-up story.

Around the late 1950's, during road construction in the Euphrates Valley of south-east Turkey, many tombs were uncovered containing the remains of giants. At the sites some leg bones were measured to be 120 cms (47.24 inches). Joe Taylor, Director of Mt. Blanco Fossil Museum, was commissioned to sculpt the human femur. This giant stood some 14-16 ft tall.

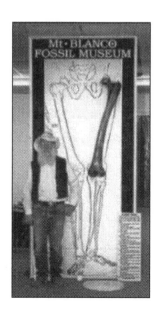

Deuteronomy 3:11 states that the bed of Og, king of Bashan, was 9 cubits by 4 cubits (approximately 14 ft long by 6 ft wide). Several accounts of giant human skeletons or depictions have been discovered from Egypt, Italy, Patagonia in Argentina, and the western US.

The largest humans in recent history like Robert Wadlow of Alton, IL (who was just under 9ft tall) who died in 1940 shows that giant people are capable of living.

Also after the fall of man, as I've written, death began to rule in human beings. But at that time humans lived hundreds of years, until God shortened mans life span even more (Genesis 6: 3-4). That is why when remains of human skeletons which date back to these times are studied it is revealed they were from people who were hundreds of years old when they died. Some doctors have extensively studied bones like these and concluded that, based upon both cranial measurements and tooth enamel wear the estimated age of death would be 250-300 years old.

Let's continue through the track of truth left by the round wheel. I've already explained about creation, Mans' fall (sin) and deception via the fallen angels and many more things that show the history of the earth and truth about the world. But there is so much more to add; for instance if you remember when I wrote about the Tower of Babel which was built after the flood, well after that time the earth's population as previously stated was divided and scattered by God. He made visual divides in appearance and language and man-kind wandered to inhabit the earth in groups. All these groups were descendants of Noah's three sons and their wives (Noah was saved with his family from the flood on the ark, also many animals, as previously explained). The names of those three sons was Shem, Ham and Japheth and all the nations on earth right up till the present day are descendants of those three. The Bible explains all this clearly (Genesis: 10 1-32). So here is the basic layout which man has dispersed from starting with:

Ham = (Hamitic) Africa & Arabia.
Ethiopians, Libyans, Phoenician's & Canaanites, Jebusite, Amorite, Girgasite.

Shem = (Semitic) Assyria.
Persians, Assyrians, Chaldeans, Armenians, Syrians....etc

Japheth = (Japhetic) Asia Minor & Europe.
Gauls, Britons, Germans, Russians, Medes, Iberians, Greeks, Romans, Thracians etc.

This shows the historic structure of humanity to this day. Here is the history of the world in your hands. There is so much more to this but I don't want to overload you with too much information.

You see, the Bible gives total insight to the history of the earth. God wants people to know these things so they can see the truth. Nothing else explains history like this, because nothing else can. Anything else is a lie that can make no sense. This is just the tip of the 'iceberg' as to how the Bible gives truthful layout and structure to the past, present and future.

Sodom and Gomorrah

When God scattered human beings by giving them different languages at the Tower of Babel (as mentioned), they wandered around the earth in huge groups looking for places to settle. One group of those people settled in a valley in Jordan and also the Valley of Siddim, and they built cities there over time. But the people of these cities became very bad and committed a lot of immoral and perverse sin, apart from much other sin. But there was a man named Lot who lived there. He suffered day after day the pain of living with immoral and lawless people. But God saw him and decided he would save him and his family but destroy the cities completely. So God sent two angels into the city where Lot lived so that he could be warned and escape before the cities were destroyed. Lot told his other relatives about what was going to happen but they thought he was only joking. By the help of the angels Lot escaped, but many others who did not obey and listen to God's truth remained in the cities. When Lot was some distance away burning sulphur rained down on the cities and the smoke from them went up like a huge furnace. The cities were completely destroyed and through time that area went on to become part of the Dead Sea, which is there today. The Dead Sea is full of salt, and nothing lives in it at all. In fact there is so much salt in it that you can float in the water. God has made it this way to represent death and the hellish consequence of not obeying his righteous ways. The Bible also mentions a lot of teachings that relate to salt: it has Biblical meaning. That is also why we have the word 'Sodomy' which relates to unnatural and perverse sexual sin. This comes from the name of one of the cities.

There has been explorations of the Dead Sea, during which the remains of Sodom and Gomorrah were found (that is bits and pieces which have been melted in what has been described as a massive amount of heat, that of a nuclear bomb).

All this shows the realism and remains of the events of the Bible and how they have shaped the whole course of the world.

Near the Dead Sea are many mountains, and not so long ago a young boy found Biblical writings relating to some of the great events of the Bible written by Isaiah (A great prophet of the Bible) in some of the caves. These scrolls and writings went on to be known as the Dead Sea Scrolls.

<u>You can see that the track left by the round wheel is perfect, but it still keeps going with no breaks at all</u>.

Anyway around this time there was another man called Abraham. He was chosen by God to be the 'Father of many nations' as he was promised many children. God accepted this man as righteous because he believed in him and as a sign to show this he was circumcised. From then on until around the time of Jesus Christ's resurrection, circumcision was performed on all males. It is common knowledge to understand that circumcision is to do with the Jews and the Old Testament. Jewish people are the descendants of Abraham. These people went on to live in the land of Israel, which of course is still there today.

So as just explained God puts right with himself everyone who believes in him, but because we now know about Jesus Christ we have to believe in him to believe in God.

At the time of Abraham Jesus Christ had not yet come into the world so God overlooked peoples' wrongdoing until the time of Christ when all sin would be dealt with once and for all by his sacrifice on the cross. That is why the Bible talks about faith a lot because it is by your faith in Jesus Christ that you become right with God. God puts right with himself <u>anyone</u> who believes in Christ no matter what they have or have not done, as long as they try to live a good and holy life. So there is no need to be circumcised like the Jews were in the Old Testament. That was just a sign to show that they were really saved by faith. So faith in Jesus Christ makes a person right with God. Faith in Jesus Christ is vital.

So Abraham was made right through faith and God gave him many descendants. Through these descendants God was accomplishing his will for humanity and as time went on these people lived in Egypt. So the next great events of the Bible happened in and around Egypt. The Bible has much detail of events that took place in and around Egypt, at that time, which have significant and powerful meanings that have shaped the whole course of the world up to this day. This is found in the Bible under the book of Exodus.

So Abraham's sons were having children of their own and increasing in number. One of those sons was Isaac, (another strong Biblical figure). One of Isaac's sons was Jacob (again a strong Biblical figure). Jacob had twelve sons who formed Israel. Then these people went to occupy part of the land of Egypt. They became so numerous and strong that Egypt was filled with them.

Now everyone has heard about Egypt but a lot of people fail to see the truth behind it, which is all Biblically accounted for. The history involved with the Egyptians is linked to the history of the Israelites and the Bible.....of course.

When the Israelites went into the land of Egypt they were accepted by the Egyptians and were allowed to settle in a part of Egypt called Goshen and they became more numerous than the people of Egypt. But then a new Egyptian King came into power and he ignored God and worshipped his own 'god'. He wanted the Israelites to decrease in number so they could never become a threat to him, even though they were a good and honest people. So he put slave-drivers over them to crush their spirits with hard work. The

Egyptians feared the great number of Israelites and made their lives miserable by forcing them into cruel slavery, and they had no mercy on them.

<u>That is why to this day in the land of Egypt there are spectacular buildings and structures which the Israelites were forced to build in cruel slavery. This all fits in with the Bible and again shows the reality of it.</u>

After some time a boy was born among the Israelites and was adopted by the Egyptian King's daughter. This child went on to lead the Israelites out of Egypt, and God performed many incredible and unusual miracles to make this happen, because the Egyptian king would not let the people go. The name of this man was Mosses. He successfully lead the people out of Egypt with God's help and also lead the people through the Red Sea. Many people have heard of the events of Moses and the parting of the Red Sea but many people fail to see the reality of it which is a <u>fatal mistake</u> to make about the historical truth of the world. These events shaped the whole course and structure of humanity, but people are becoming too pre-occupied with their lives and are not looking and studying the truth. People are ultimately neglecting the most important events of humanity.

After Moses came out of Egypt the Israelites had been there 430 years. God gave him the regulations about the Passover, which is a festival recognized to this day. Then God lead the people through the Red Sea, which is a symbol pointing to baptism. That is why people get baptized to this day. It is all symbolic and represents God being part of your life through Christ.

So in this new land God gave Moses the Ten Commandments, which to this day are partly used in some government systems of law and order, although many people do not see the foundation from which they came. The Bible has really set into motion the fundamental laws of society but now many of those laws have been twisted, corrupted and changed by man and new untruthful laws added in their place. God is ultimately being cancelled out.

The place where Moses received the Ten Commandments was a mountain called Mount Sinai. There has been an alter found in this region just as the Bible describes with twelve uncut stones.

The Ten Commandments are as follows:

1. Worship no God but the Lord.
2. Do not make any images of anything in heaven or on earth or in the water under the earth. Do not bow down to <u>any idol</u> or worship it.
3. Do not misuse the Lord's name.
4. Observe the Sabbath and keep it holy. You have six days to do your work but the seventh is a day of rest dedicated to me.
5. Respect your father and mother.
6. Do not commit murder.
7. Do not commit adultery.
8. Do not steal.
9. Do not accuse anyone falsely.
10. Do not desire another man's wife, or anything else he owns.

Some of these laws are in use in society to this day. Yet people fail to see where they came from!

God gave many other laws and instructions to Man and again they are common practice to this day. For instance God commanded that no-one is to have sexual relations with their relatives. Early in Man's history (nearer creation) there were no laws for such things as these. Sexual activity was different but it was not perverse because God had not condemned certain ways in which we would act by giving a law.

Then God gave these regulations: (Leviticus 17: 6-18)

Do not disgrace your father by having intercourse with your mother. Do not disgrace your own mother.

Do not have intercourse with your sister or step-sister. Do not have intercourse with your granddaughter. Do not have intercourse with a half sister: she is your sister.

Do not have intercourse with an aunt, or your uncle's wife; she, too, is your aunt.

Do not have intercourse with your daughter-in-law or your brother's wife.

Do not have intercourse with the daughter or granddaughter of a woman with whom you have had intercourse.

The regulations go into detail and this detail is still strongly used in the world today. <u>This is where it came from</u>! The Bible - Gods word and sound instruction. Many people all over the world know that having sexual relations with your relatives is wrong but they don't understand exactly why. The answer is from the laws that were given to Moses from God when the Israelites were lead out of Egypt.

<u>So there you have it. People obey God's laws yet they don't believe in him?</u>! This just shows how mixed up people are and demonstrates that people aren't thinking clearly.

Soap operas on television thrive on controversial issues such as incest, immorality and other wrongdoing yet they display no foundation from which these things originated. Ultimately programs like this make out that everyday life has no Biblical connection. They numb peoples' minds to what is wrong and smash God's word of truth, mixing people up all the time and making sin appear cool and trendy. They also spread gossip and all kinds of wrongful desires to people.

Certain divorce and marriage regulations again came from this event. However when Christ came into the world he gave new teachings about divorce (Matthew 5: 31-32), but they too are being treated with neglect and lack of respect for God. People can think there is nothing wrong with divorcing there husband or wife on any grounds - that it is just part of life. But the teachings of Christ stand and there are many people doing the wrong thing.

One of the major parts of peoples' ignorance and defiance is that they don't fear God. This is a terrible mistake to make.

The Bible clearly states that God is full of love and mercy but he is also mighty and extremely powerful; in fact there is no limit to his power. The Bible also states that God is someone you <u>must fear</u>. The simple fact is that people do not know who they are messing with in their defiance and ignorance. The Bible actually explains that in the future God will totally destroy and melt in a raging inferno the whole universe by his <u>presence</u>. This clearly shows God is extremely powerful.

So there is much that could be written about God's laws that were given to Moses, that in turn shape peoples' lives today, yet many ignore them. In fact all over the world it is seen as fun to pour scorn and dishonour to what God has said is holy. For example: in Las Vegas people get married as a kind of fancy dress party and pay no homage to God, and the so-called priest is dressed up as a dead Rock star.

Also in certain parts of the world men get married to men and women to women, which is all completely wrong. These people are corrupted and perverse and do not accept the truth. God wants them to do the right thing but they simply will not do it.

The list that details Man's wrongdoing and disgrace toward God is huge.

The trouble is that people forget how powerful, holy and mighty God is, and neglect his great tolerance, patience and kindness. In fact because God is kind to the wicked he is ignored and not seen as a threat! The reason God is kind and patient is because he wants all people to repent. If God did not give anything to the wicked they would hate him and because he does give they have forgotten him, only few find the balance to which God works and give him honour.

So anyway the foundation of Moses is evident to this day. After Moses got the Ten Commandments other laws were added and Moses led the people for 40 years in wilderness where God provided for them (the reasons and principles behind these events directly connect Jesus Christ to them. That is why God made them happen as they did). These people went on to Israel and there they started to build the city. There is much more substance to this but I will focus on the main events of history as not to confuse or overload you with history.

Some time later three main kings went on to rule Israel and they were King Saul, King David and King Solomon.

King Saul ruled Israel for 40 years, as did King David who as I mentioned earlier fought the Philistine giant Goliath. King David is another strong figure in history and he had great faith in God. Here is a quote from King David that shows that they were not a simple people and they saw God in what he has made, as well as the many other miracles and things he did at that time. This quote also underlines the point I was making about evolution being a 'square wheel'.

'The heavens declare the glory of God; the skies proclaim the work of his hands. Day after day they pour forth speech; night after night they display knowledge. There is no speech or language where their voice is not heard. Their voice goes out into all the earth, their words to the ends of the world.'

King David is also the one who gave us this phrase:

"As I walk through the valley of the shadow of death I will fear no evil."

Again this literature is still used today.

After King David came his son King Solomon who became very great and also ruled for 40 years. His dynasty was enormous and he built many beautiful buildings and structures. Part of the remains of King Solomon's Dynasty is still there in Israel today in Jerusalem. There are many structures and buildings that again show the clear remains of these events. Many of the wise writings of King Solomon are still used today in society, this is again failed to be seen by many. From the time of King Solomon up to the time of Jesus Christ all is recorded and accounted for in the Bible. Many things happened during that time, which have shaped the course of history and many places on earth have got their names from these events.

Anyway we reach the time where Jesus Christ is to be born. The areas Christ lived and travelled around are basically the same to this day.

Jesus Christ is an historic figure that towers above everyone else. The existence of Jesus is recorded through Palestine in his time and the governments that opposed him were very real. You must see here that Jesus was a real man who was born by God's power into the human race in order to redeem or save us from wrongdoing, all sin and death. The whole course of history was set out by God for a time he chose to bring Christ into the world (although many things have happened that are not in accordance with his will).

At Christmas time much of the world celebrates, by giving each other gifts and presents of all kinds. It's a way of showing love and kindness to one another. But as is well known, this all comes from the celebration of the birth of a man called Jesus Christ. Jesus however was not conceived and born by man and woman but rather God and woman. The Bible explains that woman was made from man i.e. Adam's rib was used by God's power round the time of creation to make women (Eve). This same power God used to bring his own son into the world by making a virgin pregnant – the virgins name was Mary. So by the power of God's own spirit he brought his son into existence in the world through a woman and he was named Jesus. The trouble is that many are failing to take Jesus Christ seriously at Christmas, and instead look at it in a purely materialistic way. The truth about Christ at Christmas time is drowned out by Santa Claus and other fairy tale concepts that cloud peoples' minds both young and old. Yet the truth about God is right under their nose! So Christmas is really a celebration of Christ yet the real meaning is pushed away, drowned out and many want to please themselves, not God.

Many people know the events that surrounded Jesus' birth and life. Many would have taken part in school plays and all sorts of religious events but as these people have grown up they have slowly forgotten all this, and sadly pushed this message aside.

One of the big problems is that no-one talks about God enough in everyday conversation (if at all). People seem to think the only place you talk about God is in a church. Another reason is people are afraid of what others think and don't want to be, as it were, singled out. Also as I explained earlier human nature and God's nature are opposed to one another, in other words people who don't know God can't know him if they subject themselves to live by their own nature and not God's. There is much insight and reason as to why these things are so, but people do not read the Bible to get that insight and knowledge. It's only when you give God a chance to show you the truth that you start to realize the Bible is completely right and true. If this book has changed the way you think about God and made you conscious of the truth, accept it because it really is the truth and should not be thrown away.

Another strong influence on peoples' minds that stops them from knowing the truth or letting it slip is sexuality. I have already mentioned this but I feel it should be underlined again. Sexuality plays a massive part in filtering out God because people can love living immoral and corrupt lives of pleasure and lust. If you live corruptly you will purposely walk away from God's message because it hinders your life style of sin, so people ignore God's message and pursue their own desires and interests. Also if a child's parents have lived like this and purposely pushed God aside then their child will grow up to ignore God and follow their human nature almost automatically. Believe me, this is what has been happening time and time again, through generations, right up to this very day.

So people can hate the message of the Bible and be opposed to it strongly, yet the truth about it is there in front of them every day.

Remember, God made sexuality but when he did we were not perverse or knowledgeable about nakedness as explained and it was all dynamically balanced by God. But Man's wrongdoing has tipped that balance and these things have become completely corrupted, twisted, warped and wrong. People talk in filthy ways and laugh at disgusting acts of behaviour. All these things aid to prevent people from accepting God's teachings.

Another thing that can hinder God's message is false interpretation of Christians. For instance many who don't believe in God can think that people who believe in Christ and the Bible are Mr or Mrs 'Perfect'. In other words they think that they are looked down on by Christians. This is totally not true. The Bible teaches that we all need Christ Jesus and are all sinners, but those who believe in him are set free and forgiven. God has made it very easy to be put right with himself: it is simply done by believing in Christ and trying to live a good and holy life. Christians are not perfect....of course, but what makes the difference is whether you try to do good and believe in Christ. So there you have it, Christians aren't trying to prove that they are superior but that really we are all the same. It's just that Christians have been forgiven, because they believe in Jesus Christ.

So if you feel this relates to you, remember what I have written previously and don't be biased to the message on the basis of human nature or anything for that matter. As explained the Bible goes right the way back in time and shows a clean truthful line of history, like the track left by the round wheel. This track comes far back from the beginning of the world (creation) to Christ and right to this very day.

Another celebration that is ignored by many for its real meaning is Easter. This is when Christ rose from the grave, and just before that Good Friday. This is when we have hot cross buns and Easter eggs, again the meaning can be ignored. Lent is another one. There are loads more that interweave into the worlds society.

<u>Any festival or celebration that does not agree with Jesus Christ being the only man who was the son of God who died for the sins of the world and who rose again three days later is a complete lie.</u> Unfortunately there are false beliefs which are complete nonsense, which again cause many to be blind to the truth.

Even our dating system is based on the birth of Christ i.e. the year 2000 marked roughly 2000 years since the birth of Christ. This is used world-wide, and again shows the impact God's son had(s) on the world...of course.

Here are some more examples of the way God has structured the truth into our lives.

Twelve has Biblical meaning, and Christ had 12 disciples.
There are the 12 tribes of Israel.
12 hours in a day
12 hours in a night.
12 months in a year.

Seven is the number of God.
There are seven spirits of God.
Seven colours of the rainbow.
Seven days in a week.

Think how much these things listed are part of your life. You are so used to them that they almost go by without being noticed. But these all originate from the first book in the Bible, Genesis. These times and principles were set into motion by God and you are living them out to this day. This shows that you and I are part of a much bigger and incredible picture.

We are all so very important and we were made by God through Christ. This truth looks at us every day. Don't be fooled by cheap 'merchandise' that has no value and no truth in it (false teachings). This world will try to force you to 'buy' poor quality 'merchandise' that is worth nothing. It is like going to a sale that you were told would be good, then when you get there you are almost forced into buying rubbish by cunning and disgraceful liars who want your money and nothing else. But because some people start buying junk other people begin to as well. Some waste all their money while others become wise to it and don't spend any more and instead they go and buy a good quality item elsewhere at a good price which becomes even more valuable, thus they make a very good investment.

The valuable item I am writing about here is the true wisdom and knowledge about God and Christ Jesus. Believe me, the truth about God is a valuable thing, in fact it is the only real thing of true value in this world.

Not having this wisdom and knowledge is incredibly dangerous. It is like a wilder beast that goes for a drink in still water. Its thirst for life hinders its wisdom because if it looked closely it would see an enormous crocodile slowly and patiently creeping up on it. This is representative of death. Then all of a sudden those still waters become furiously unsettled and the poor foolish animal is dragged under the water in the jaws of death to the darkness where it is devoured. You see, sometimes having a little wisdom and knowledge can make all the difference. It's like trying to get through a door that has a number lock on it, and if you don't get through you will die. All you need is those simple numbers. This is how it is with the truth about God: the knowledge and acceptance of Christ Jesus is all you need. But sadly many become wise to that when it is too late for them.

You must remember here that the truth about God and Christ Jesus explains all things that are part of this earth. Not one thing or small detail is left out. That is why it is the truth.

This world is like people who are walking into a cave or tunnel who loose their guide and become lost in total darkness. But God's truth is the way out and the light that comes from his truthful knowledge and wisdom gives that path. This is why God is explained in the Bible as being light and truth because this principle was created by him. You see, people are lost in darkness in principle by not having the true knowledge and wisdom which comes from God. It is all very simple but immensely powerful.

Don't be fooled. Good and evil are self-evident and the powers behind them are real......obviously. There is no excuse at all not to believe. If something stops you from acknowledging Christ Jesus in all truth, throw it away, give it up and let it go. Ignoring God is extremely dangerous.

God has made the whole of creation as an 'advertisement' that he exists, everything in creation shows this. His works are so good and obvious that some enjoy what God has made and give him glory and believe in Jesus Christ, which is all God wants. While others live for pleasure and forget him, so people ignore God because others do. People who ignore God are 'tripping up' over nothing! God has made his existence plain yet people are 'tripping' over nothing – because there is nothing that can prove he does not exist.

So as you can now see, everything points to God and Christ Jesus, and the truth about the world is all around us and fully recorded in the Bible, like a track of truth going right the way back in history. The teachings of Jesus are sound doctrine and make perfect sense in all ways. Jesus Christ was a real man who was brought into the world by God. He is the only real truth. Nothing else fits; saying that another belief is the truth is completely wrong. It's like trying to fit a square block in a round slot. It is impossible. This way of thinking has no real structure, substance or truth in it.

Remember there can only be one truth but many lies. Many people are not looking close enough. If they did they would see the Bible has no faults it is completely truthful and explains everything.

If you analyse Christ's death on the cross at Calvary you will see that it was perfectly executed and divinely planned by God. It explains how God deals with sin and the principles involved in his death make total dynamic sense. The more you read about Christ's death the more you see why it had to be that way, and how true it is!

The best thing for a person to do is read the Bible, because as I have already explained it was superhumanly written by God working through men.

Chapter 8

Overall Summary

Remember, that if you take away all the modern buildings, roads, cars, technology and every man-made thing in this world, you are left with just human beings and nature, exactly how it is described in the Bible. You are also left with two people male and female (Adam and Eve). Many think creation is a fairy tale or a story for kids.....NO indeed! People who think this way have lost track of the past history of mankind and become very confused. So the history of the earth is plain. God's creative power is also plain to understand, yet these simple fundamental facts are not being acknowledged enough. If you are still not fully convinced about God and Christ please read this next piece remembering all that has been written previously – if you do believe this summary will also be of interest to you.

Think of the miracle of childbirth. It's easy to see that childbirth is the work of a creator. If you study the incredible way a child is born you can only marvel at God's breathtaking knowledge and understanding. It is that simple to see that God is real. So let's just briefly look at pregnancy and childbirth. When my wife was pregnant she went for a scan at the hospital. Here is a picture showing the scan photo.

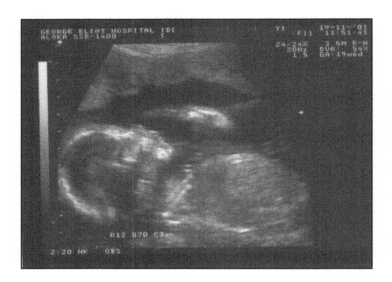

It's great to see a child like this!.....This is **Divine Natural Architecture** at work!

Then it made me think about 'clearness'. In other words this scan photo shows an incredible process happening which is immensely complex and organized yet it is depicted in a blurry, hazy, black and white image. I concluded that peoples' perception of things like pregnancy and childbirth along with God's other amazing works of creation are also depicted as hazy and blurry images in peoples' minds. In other words they think only about the outline and basic image of the created world. For example, many people take natural beauty for granted and think that's just how it is. They can see the beauty in nature and the incredible designs of God yet they don't see his image. Many just see what they want to see. So all the complex structures that show God's Divine Natural Architecture are not linked to God. People ignore God and do not give him the high honour that belongs to him. They forget how incredible creation actually is and over time that Godly knowledge becomes black and white and looses its clarity, just like the scan image. It's extremely important not to forget, ignore or overlook the importance and sheer obviousness of creation. It's a bit like buying a book, then eventually forgetting the author who wrote it. Society is fast becoming too busy and the world is losing focus on the true, clear image of God displayed in nature. Much of the world has completely ignored and forgotten that God made the human race. This is of vital importance and we should never become 'retired' to this plain fact.

The truth about God is a great thing that will give you true happiness.

So here is just a glimpse of the truth, which clearly shows God's divine knowledge and power in creation.

The structure of DNA consists of a series of units called nucleotides. Each nucleotide is made up of deoxyribose, a phosphate group, and several nitrogenous bases (adenine, thymine, guanine, and cytosine). Phosphate groups bond to an adjacent carbon atom, forming a polynucleotide chain. The DNA of most living organisms have two of these chains twisted together forming a double helix. The DNA in this double helix is packed up extremely well in a complex, efficient and elegant way. Such a large molecule is not fully stretched out inside the cell, but is wound around proteins called histones which protect the DNA. The double helix formation of DNA is coated by a sugar-phosphate sequence. The nitrogenous bases are attracted to those of another chain by hydrogen bonds. Adenine is always linked by two hydrogen bonds to thymine, and guanine is attached to cytosine by three hydrogen bonds.

These nucleotides are commonly abbreviated by their first letter (e.g. A, C, G, T). One of the strands is called the sense (note: truth=sense) and the other strand is called the anti-sense. This sequence of codes is incredibly small and extremely complex. (Note: much of our D.N.A is not understood).

The first step in reading the information stored within DNA is a process called transcription. Before transcription the D.N.A is opened up and the double helix structure is 'unwound'. This is done by breaking the weak links to open up the chemical code. During transcription, enzymes within the cell use nucleotides to replicate a specific segment of the sense DNA strand. However, it is not a perfect replication. In the replication strand, all of the Thymine nucleotides are replaced with uricle nucleotide's, which are nearly chemically identical. The replicated segment of DNA is called ribonucleic acid or RNA.

The RNA then leaves the nucleus and enters the cytoplasm where it is parsed by a ribosome. This parsing process is called translation, (also known as decoding). The RNA nucleotides are grouped into 3's, called a codon. Because there are four different base pairs grouped into threes, there are 64 possible codons. Three of the 64 codons correspond to punctuation and the remaining 61 correspond to about 20 amino acids.

The RNA is a complementary copy of one strand of the DNA. The RNA leaves the nucleus and in the cytoplasm (outer part of cell) it is translated into a protein. Each set of three RNA nucleotides codes for a single amino acid, and the protein is made of a chain of amino acids linked to one another. So each set of three nucleotides in the DNA eventually codes for one amino acid in the final protein that is made from a given gene. The nucleotides and amino acids are not similar chemically, and it is the protein synthesis machinery of the cell that is needed to translate one code into the other. This shows that the cell and D.N.A were perfectly designed for one another. The resultant proteins may be further processed and packaged within the cell or be ready for action as enzymes, structural elements, antibodies or hormones. Enzymes control other complex chemical reactions within the cell, which all works beautifully.

I have collectively written this information to try to demonstrate to you how complex and incredible life is. This information however is just the beginning to understanding life, and even then it has been simplified and parts are missing otherwise it would be too much to take in. I haven't even begun to mention many other complex parts of the cell and complete chromosome formation......etc.......etc, let alone the incredible journey of the sperm and many, many other things that make this possible!

You must realize there is no excuse not to believe in God. Ignoring his works is extremely stupid. God has made his existence plain for all to see. Remember you can't see God directly but you can see his works.

If all the chemical 'letters' in the human body were printed in books page by page, it is estimated they would fill the Grand Canyon fifty times!

A fertilized human egg is very small. To see it properly you need a microscope. Yet it contains information equivalent to billions and billions of 'chemical letters'. This is enough information to fill 1000 books, 500 pages thick with print so small you would not be able to see it. Instead you would need a microscope to read it!

The human mind is far complex than anything known. A super computer is a yo-yo in comparison. The very existence of human beings shows the existence of God.

D.N.A is God's very own 'handwriting'. There it is in front of the world's eyes! Think of it as an unknown language written down that explains how to build a human being, but none can read it, so it has to be worked out piece by piece. That is <u>exactly</u> what D.N.A is (Divine Natural Architecture).

We, and all life, are created and finished to perfection by God. Make no mistakes about it, we are amazingly made. Think of our skeletal structure and the muscle formation over it - it is an engineering masterpiece. No machine on earth can copy human movement and balance in full. All these things are perfectly linked to our minds and we are so well made that we don't really think of ourselves as 'mechanical'. Think of all bones in the body, the rib cage, skull, hands and feet etc. They are all so well 'carved' and designed. The structure of the human hand is incredible! Even the way we stand and sit is so well thought out! Think of our ears and eyes and the complex way we speak, the way we enjoy and eat food to keep us alive and the way our innards are constructed is pure genius.

Can bones 'carve' themselves? Can muscle think for itself? Can those things that make up the body be the designers of the body?......Of course not. Are people really this blind? - God is the designer.

Think of the human mind and the way we are attracted to certain forms of beauty and colour and how we are attracted to one another.

Remember that if a person likes a particular thing, it is because the human mind has been designed to like it. How can we like something we have not been designed to like? (unless a person becomes perverse). Everything has been designed by God, even the principle of design itself. Nothing can exist without the understanding of God in the first place. All life comes from God.

Think about it this way - people can be afraid of spiders - that is because God has designed into the human mind the ability to be 'disturbed' by that shape. Which, believe you me, is an extremely complex process! Also, why do men find women attractive? Simple, because they are designed that way and so to have women been designed to find men attractive. It does not just happen rather it is a process that happens in the mind which has been designed incredibly well. Another point to remember here is that a human being is a masterpiece just by looking externally, let alone the inner qualities of construction.

The Godly knowledge about creation and Jesus Christ is the most important information in the world. The trouble is, much of society does not hold any real value to such understanding. Much of the world runs on so-called knowledge that is related to money, self gain and having pleasure. People are 'trained' to think about such knowledge as useless and unimportant, yet it is the foundation of this truth that holds the key to the knowledge of God and his son Jesus Christ. The world is being brain-washed to miss the obvious! It is so simple! They are being distracted just as they start to get warm. It's like looking for some keys: many people end up finding them in the most obvious of places but look in all the places that don't make any sense or are not obvious. Yet they were right under their nose all the time (creation). Another thing that stops a person looking in the right place is other people saying they looked yet they did not really find anything (false teachings).

Also fear can stop the search for truth. For example, many people don't mention or discuss the truth about God because they are afraid of what others will think about them. So for the sake of 'fitting in' they can forget God and kid themselves and others.

People can think it is strong to be reckless and to ignore anything to do with God, Jesus Christ and creation. But really they are displaying a weakness that is wrongly interpreted as tough!

So D.N.A is the 'writing' of God. Not only is this power shown in human beings, but all creatures from the biggest to the smallest and also plant life of all kinds. The list is endless. Think of this book in all its complexity. Do you think for a moment that it wrote itself? Now try to image how complex D.N.A is. D.N.A is not just a few strands of material that happens to do something over time. As described it is far, far beyond the technology of this world. It is the ultimate super, super, super code!

When I was studying at College I built a life-size 3 dimensional figure of a man, and I can tell you that making such a thing was obviously down to understanding, skill and workmanship! Not one person who saw that figure thought it made itself! So why do they think this about themselves? This evolutionary way of thinking is causing the <u>whole</u> <u>world</u> to believe a lie, which leads to other insane debates. One of which being euthanasia which has foundations in evolution. Euthanasia is basically the killing of people who want to end their lives due to medical reasons. It is completely wrong and is not in any way justified. The people who are ill should be told the truth about God and put their faith in him. God is able to heal and that is very real. But unfortunately many people are trapped in a world of doubt and disbelief in God. They think it is nonsense to put your hope in God and that ultimately nothing will come out of it. So instead they put all their hope and trust in medical science alone and live in fear. Also many people who believe in God can lack strong faith in such matters and as a result they crumble under little pressure. There are many people today who are weak in faith and only conform to the outer part of the Bible and reject its real power. It is vital to remember that God made all things and healing the body is no challenge to him. When someone is ill many people don't even consider God as an option, rather men. To have faith in God is to consider God's healing power in everyday conversation, but instead people are afraid to bring it up! They don't want to look foolish.......far from it!

That is how God's wisdom is regarded in this world as foolish! But really it is wiser than human wisdom, and God's power is stronger than human strength!

A while ago in America the twin towers of the World Trade Centre complex were destroyed by commercial airliners flying into them, exploding and then causing the buildings to totally collapse. Not one person thought that this total chaos and disorder would do anything but destroy on a big scale. So why is it that people believe they came from the chaos, disorder and nonsense of evolution? When the twin towers fell, no one thought that in the process they would become better constructions.....of course not! Yet the strange thing is that many people who saw that terrible disaster would have believed in the theory of evolution and not given their belief a second thought. This disaster underlines much of the world's stupidity. People know full well that they are far better built, designed and engineered than these two towers were. Yet they believe the same principles that tore them down are the principles that constructed them. Even if the twin towers took thousands of years to decay they would not become better constructions. Time has nothing to do with it. So why think the same about life on this planet and the human body! Time is irrelevant but <u>creation is relevant</u>. The facts are that people are in such a mess that they don't even realize how stupid evolution is.

Man-made items are thought up, designed and made, using human skill. Most man-made things have lines of symmetry. In other words, we make things so that they are structurally balanced and beautiful. For example, if you take most man-made objects and draw a line down the centre, you will see that they fit each other when 'folded'. This way of designing things is not just something that happens. Rather, we have been designed to make things that way. This same principle is seen in nature, which shows again the works of a creator. Look at the human body: it has a line of symmetry down the middle; also flowers, leaves and many, many, many other created things. Some flowers are curled up but if you uncurl them you see they are symmetrical shapes rolled up. One of the best examples is a butterfly, with their beautiful markings. This again shows the creative power of God. Creation is not all irregular shapes and non-uniform markings. So the fact that much of creation is symmetrical shows '<u>double</u>' that God has designed all things!

Looking at man-made things shows the works of men. But in all fairness God made man and gave mankind understanding, so really anything that a man makes is really in a sense the work of God.

So all created things show balance, form, mathematical order and structure that comes together perfectly. Like paintings by great and talented artists that show perfect composition and structure, that are balanced with curvilinear formations and other shapes. The works of art in nature all demonstrate this too. Ultimately the art of nature is the best of all. People take God's <u>works of art</u> for granted and become numb to his creative display that is all around! Many travel all over the world to see paintings and sculptures of all kinds but they do not have the simple yet extremely powerful insight to see that they themselves are the greatest works of art on earth!

In the Bible it clearly explains about God making Man, and as previously told it is all true. The Bible also says that when God passed judgement onto the human race because of sin (Genesis 3: 19) he said "You were made from soil, and you will become soil again."

To this day that is exactly what happens to us all. Or is God being too plain?

God is not an all mysterious figure that cannot be understood! Far from it, God is plain and has made his divine presence plain.

Life is a <u>miracle</u>. Here are some passages from the Bible which show God's works and power over all things.

Job 39: 14-18

"The ostrich leaves her eggs on the ground for the soil to warm them. She is unaware that a foot may crush them or a wild animal break them. She acts as though the eggs were not hers, and is unconcerned that her efforts were wasted.

It was I who made her foolish and did not give her wisdom. But when she runs she can laugh at any horse and rider."

Job 36: 22-23

"Remember how great is God's power; he is the greatest teacher of all. No one can tell God what to do or accuse him of evil."

Psalms 138:13-15

"You created every part of me; you put me together in my mother's womb. I praise you because you are to be feared; all you do is strange and wonderful. I know it with all my heart. When my bones were being formed, carefully put together in my mothers womb, when I was growing there in secret, you knew that I was there - you saw me before I was born."

Luke 12:27

"Not even king Solomon with all his wealth had clothes as beautiful as one of these flowers."

A flower shows love and delicate beauty that is tender and kind, also the fragrance from a flower has these dynamic qualities too. It is these qualities in nature that are used on valentines day for example. Flowers are given to show affection and love. This is really part of God's display of love for humanity. A flower almost speaks the words "Trust in me, I love you."

It cannot be denied.

God's voice is soft and quiet yet it is loud and all around us - his voice is in nature. All created things show God's wisdom. They proclaim his glory. The story of Christ is in nature and the basis of wisdom and knowledge are displayed in the things God has made. His 'sculptures' are all around us and they show his eternal power and divine majesty. All things were made through Christ (the word of God). God, through Christ, created heaven and earth and all that is in them, of the things seen and unseen. Day and night his works proclaim his greatness, and all can see this yet many ignore God and neglect his power, mercy, and love. The world judges by its own rules and values. People say "Where is God? There is no God."

Yet God's presence is displayed in humanity itself. That is why God made Man in his image.

So it is vital to fully analyse worldly values because they have a powerful affect that stops people accepting God. For example: people can act extremely differently when others are watching, simply because they base their mindset and values in life on what others think and whether or not they fit in with the majority. So the world is caught up in judgements that are founded from human values like outward appearances, status and gossip. This happens all over the world everyday and has to be one of the most powerful tools of manipulation in this world. If you base your judgements on what others think, you're not thinking for yourself. If people do what their human nature wants then they want to fit in with human nature, not the nature of God. The trouble is that people who act this way cannot understand the actions of people who believe in the Bible because their evaluation is not based on true knowledge and God's nature. So their conclusion is influenced by what others think of them, and not what the truth is. Truth is based on God alone and Christ, and from that a person evaluates all things and then comes to a truthful conclusion. In other words if you base what you think on worldly values there can be no real truth in you. But if you base what you think on God and Christ you are truthful. That is because everything that is true points to God and Christ.

So, as now clearly seen, the whole of society can run on how people want to be portrayed and not on truth, and it gets to the stage where people don't question their actions at all and live according to their nature. People don't question where the human race came from or where it is going. They like to think they control their own lives totally and think highly of themselves (people like to think of themselves as self made 'men of the world' as it were). Some consider Christians as weak and foolish. God has made it so that to follow him you have to become humble in spirit, but many hate this and cannot cope with being humble. Christ said "Those who make themselves great will be humbled and those who humble themselves will be made great."

Christ meant this if you humble yourself because you are his follower.

Let's remember here that God is perfect and we are obviously not, so the way God makes you right with himself is by believing in Christ Jesus. When you do this and follow his teachings you will be doing good in God's sight. God makes good people perfect through their faith in Christ. So then, understand and believe what the Bible says if you do not already!

So it is foolish to use so-called worldly 'knowledge' that does not work like the square wheel. Rather, use the truthful knowledge of God and creation, the round wheel.

Full Circle

Remember earlier in the book I wrote about the truth being a long bicycle track through the earth, which made a clean line from the very beginning up to this very moment. It is now time for you to 'get on' (if you have not already) and travel in the faith of God and Christ through the rest of your life, using the round wheels of truth. No more square wheeled nonsense.

I hope that I've convinced you about God and Jesus Christ, as it is plain to see that it is completely true. Really, you have no excuse not to believe. Don't give in to wanting to please human nature through immorality and other wrongful ways, instead get on this bike of truth and pedal for yourself.

The journey of belief in the Bible is like cycling uphill. It can be difficult but not impossible. There are many who are against God and ignore his truthful teaching because they don't look into his ways with the right heart and they don't examine how it all works. To examine the right way of God you have to read the Bible, which will give you the strength to cycle on wheels of truth, all the way home.

So I simply leave the rest to you. I've sown the seed.

The purpose of this book is to show the truth about the world in a very clear, plain and effective way, thus helping people from being confused about many issues. It also shows that the truth to all things is not hard to understand i.e. the obviousness of creation - and that the Bible explains all questions that are needed to show it is the truth and why God has done the things he has. It also shows that belief in Christ is essential to God's plan for humanity and it explains why many people ignore God's message because it is opposed to human nature.

So remember what you have read in this book and apply it to your life, remembering that in the basket of that bicycle is the Bible. For it to be effective you must read it often and learn from it. Thank you for reading this book.

If you are already a Christian I'm sure this book will have helped to explain, underline and clear the mind about many worldly problems. It is a privilege to have been able to bring these words to you. Thanks for reading.

(Please pass this book on, and keep the truthful wheel turning)

Christ Jesus said "Anyone who does what is right and believes in me will receive eternal life."
He also said "I came to give life in all its fullness."

All created things were made by God through Christ, who died and rose again for the sins of humanity. D.N.A shows God's Divine Natural Architecture.

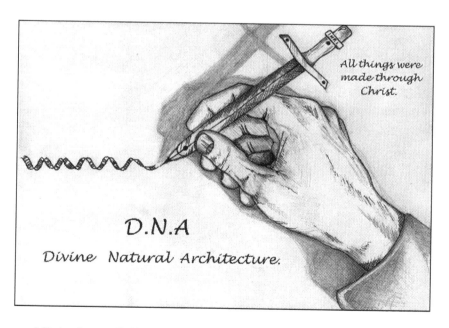

All the best, Colin Campbell-Barker.

(A special thanks to Theo Campbell-Barker and Neville Campbell-Barker with their help in the editing of this book.)